RAGE AGAINST THE SYSTEM

AN EXPOSÉ ON THE LIES OF SOCIETY

A. P. HOVSEPIAN

Copyright © A. P. Hovsepian

All rights reserved.

No part of this publication may be reproduced, stored or transmitted in any form or by any means, electronic, mechanical, photocopying, recording, scanning, or otherwise without written permission from the publisher. It is illegal to copy this book, post it to a website, or distribute it by any other means without permission.

The author is not responsible for the persistence or accuracy of URLs for external or third-party Internet Websites referred to in this publication and does not guarantee that any content on such Websites is, or will remain, accurate or appropriate.

Designations used by companies to distinguish their products are often claimed as trademarks. All brand names and product names used in this book and on its cover are trade names, service marks, trademarks and registered trademarks of their respective owners. The publishers and the book are not associated with any product or vendor mentioned in this book. None of the companies referenced within the book have endorsed the book.

CONTENTS

The System Has You	1
1. Diamonds Are Worthless	7
2. Marriage Is Toxic	20
3. Employees Are Losers	36
4. School Is Child Abuse	54
5. Passion Is Overrated	73
6. Charity Is Perverse	96
7. Common Sense Is Nonexistent	114
This Is Your Last Chance	142
Notes	153

THE SYSTEM HAS YOU

You have to understand: Most of these people are not ready to be unplugged. And many of them are so inured, so hopelessly dependent on the system, that they will fight to protect it.

— Morpheus

WHAT IS THE SYSTEM?

The system is the unwritten rules of civilization. It is the invisible script of life we adopt through osmosis, embrace with conviction, and obey without question.

The system is the subdued state of society. It is the psychological stronghold on the general population; the mental confines we are born into.

. . .

The system is the credulous condition of humanity. It is the world that has been pulled over our eyes, in order to blind us from the truth.

The system has lulled us into a perennial state of ignorance and passivity. It has tamed potential trailblazers, pioneers and revolutionaries. The pain it has inflicted, the prosperity it has destroyed, and the progress it has stifled is simply incalculable.

The system must be openly challenged, defied and exposed. There is too much at stake to allow it to persist. The time has come to dismantle the system, in all the ways it has manifested in the world. In order to do that, we must first ask ourselves a pointed question: *do I suffer from the Semmelweis reflex?*

Most people do. The Semmelweis reflex is the cerebral phenomenon of immediately rejecting any new idea that challenges your existing way of thinking about certain ideas or objects. The term is derived from Doctor Ignaz Semmelweis, who in 1847 discovered that childbed fever mortality rates fell by 10x when doctors disinfected their hands in between patients[1]. His fellow colleagues and contemporaries rejected the idea, however, despite the overwhelming evidence of its effectiveness. They could not accept the notion that their hands could transmit disease. As a result, they remained in their ignorance, causing several avoidable deaths in the process[2].

. . .

Some portions of this text may challenge the preconceived notions you have held onto for an extended period of life. As you navigate the pages ahead, be ever aware of the cognitive inertia — the Semmelweis reflex — that may arise within. And should such a moment of dissension present itself, to the point of outrage or indignation, I urge you to continue reading; not for any other reason than to prevent a sole contention from impeding potential breakthrough further along. Pragmatically, absorb the useful and discard the redundant. Metaphorically, eat the meat and spit out the bones.

Whether or not you consider yourself curious, cautious or skeptical, we have all fallen victim to various forms of indoctrination, herd mentality, groupthink and general misinformation fed to us by the system. Thus, it is no small feat to recognize and resist bias that has been ingrained within us for a prolonged period of time. That said, it is entirely possible to do so, given an open mind and earnest inclination for the truth.

May you explore the forthcoming pages with honest inquiry. May it produce clarity in your perspective and successive reality. May this letter be the first step on your journey of deliverance from the constraints of the system.

HOW TO READ THIS BOOK

Each chapter is independent of the other. There is no sequential order. You may turn to any at your discretion, as you see fit.

There is no need to rush or skim. For the sake of efficiency, effectiveness and your valuable time, brevity has been implemented at every turn. No sentence has been included that could be considered unnecessary or open to abridgment. Great strides have been made to ensure this book is as short and concise as possible, not allowing for a point to be lost in obscurity, fluff or filler. French mathematician and philosopher, Blaise Pascal, has been attributed the statement, "*I have made this letter longer than usual, because I have not had time to make it shorter*"[3]. I tremble at the thought of ever making such a declaration.

I wrote this book for the 18-year-old version of me. This is the manual I wish I had when I was entering adulthood. As a result, it will naturally appeal to younger men, considering most issues arose from the various challenges and hardships I personally endured. That being said, I have made an attempt to some extent to ensure it is beneficial to all who read it.

Lastly, please gift me with your honest thoughts and suggestions when you have reached the end. The details are in the afterword.

. . .

Without further delay, let's dive in, and see how deep this rabbit hole goes...

1

DIAMONDS ARE WORTHLESS

Diamonds are intrinsically worthless.

— Nicky Oppenheimer

WHY DO YOU ASCRIBE VALUE TO A DIAMOND?

Diamonds are a $79 billion-dollar industry[1]. Despite market crashes, geopolitical sanctions, economic recessions and global pandemics, it retains universal appeal, with popularity remaining fairly consistent over the years and decades. The simplest explanation for this is also the plausible one: its value is tethered to perception, not reality.

Most of us perceive diamonds to be unequivocally rare pieces of jewelry. We're inclined to purchase them during the wedding process because, among other things, they are a symbol of love. And even if things turn sour in our relationships, we can still see the ring as an investment. Right?

Wrong. On all accounts.

Diamonds are not at all what we may think they are. Evidence suggests their market positioning derives from a tactful combination of monopoly, ignorance and clever marketing. And while this information is nothing new, the general population remains relatively oblivious to the embellished, inflated and deceitfully overstated worth of a diamond.

DIAMONDS ARE NOT RARE

You may have simply assumed diamonds are expensive and desirable due to their scarcity.

Diamonds are not rare. They are anything but. Compared to other gemstones, diamonds are the most common precious stone in the world[2]. There are more diamonds in the world than we know what to do with. That's right: supply exceeds demand.

In fact, diamonds are *so* common that, as of 1982, it was estimated that some 100 million women were wearing diamonds in some fashion, with millions more packing them away in safe-deposit boxes[3]. It was further estimated the public held more than 500 million carats of diamonds at the time. Shockingly, this was all before the Argyle mine in Western Australia even came into the picture. In operation since 1983, this mine has produced over 800 million carats of diamonds[4].

With these kinds of numbers, we would expect to see widespread abundance of diamonds, along with a steep drop in diamond prices. But that would not be good for those in the diamond business. It just wouldn't make sense to flood the market with more rocks. Thus, the impulse to impede supply was conceived.

. . .

Here was the billion dollar question: how difficult would it be to convince the entire diamond industry to be unified on this one ambitious idea? Evidently, not too difficult at all! As it turns out, a single company controlled the diamond supply chain for most of the 20th century.

In operation since 1888, the corporation known as *De Beers* owns most of the diamond mines around the world. And the mines they don't own, they've historically bought out all their inventory, intimidating or co-opting any that think of resisting their monopoly.

Keeping the diamond supply contained is also what kept it valuable. By buying out several diamond mines and controlling output, one company restricted the majority supply of diamonds, projecting a sense of rarity and artificially boosting the perceived value of a diamond onto the public square. The founder himself, Cecil Rhodes, communicated to his shareholders in 1896, *"the only risk is the sudden discovery of new mines, which human nature will work recklessly to the detriment of us all"*[5].

We've been swayed by the sparkle of false scarcity, for a piece of crystallized carbon that's worth virtually nothing. Indeed, there will never be a shortage of diamonds on this planet. If anything, we're being overwhelmed by their ubiquity. Thanks to technology, diamonds are being discovered at even faster rates.

. . .

Diamonds are now being dredged en masse from the seabed along the Namibian coastline in South Africa, with custom-built diamond mining vessels crawling the ocean floor. 24 hours a day. 7 days a week[6].

And it doesn't stop there. Diamonds are also being created in labs. Lockheed Martin filed a patent for a 3D printer that prints diamonds[7]. The Diamond Foundry, a startup, has raised hundreds of millions of dollars in early-stage venture rounds from the likes of Obvious Ventures, Mark Pincus (Zynga) and Leonardo DiCaprio[8], making synthetic diamonds branded as unique to the core with one-of-a-kind inclusions and unique growth patterns.

Don't be fooled: there are entire warehouses all around the world, full of diamonds, waiting to be sold.

DIAMONDS ARE NOT ROMANTIC

The popular practice of marking an engagement with a diamond ring is nothing more than a shrewd marketing invention. A fairly recent one, at that.

Prior to the early 1950s, there was no psychological connection between diamonds and marriage. During that period of time, diamond sales were slow. That was, until the De Beers company finally decided to do something about it.

In 1938, they hired an advertising agency called 'N.W. Ayer'. A copywriter by the name of Mary Frances Gerety was assigned to the De Beers account. She recalls a De Beers representative writing to inquire about "*the use of propaganda in various forms*" to help sell more diamonds[9]. The agency proceeded to conduct consumer surveys. They quickly uncovered the heart of the issue: most of the general population just didn't want diamond rings.

Ayer found that many believed diamonds were "money down the drain". Gerety recalls consumers were largely of the opinion the money would be better spent on "a washing machine, or a new car"[10]. They were desperately trying to promote a product that people didn't want, nor could they afford.

The solution? Promote diamonds as a symbol of love.

Ayer stressed the need to strengthen the association in the public's mind of diamonds with romance, concluding *"it would be crucial to inculcate in men the idea that diamonds were a gift of love: the larger and finer the diamond, the greater the expression of love. Similarly, young women had to be encouraged to view diamonds as an integral part of any romantic courtship"*[11]. They had found their angle.

"We are dealing with a problem in mass psychology", they declared. The agency planned to *"strengthen the tradition of the diamond engagement ring — to make it a psychological necessity"*[12]. Within 3 years, despite the Great Depression, diamond sales in the U.S. increased by 55%[13]. Ayer also organized a number of talks at schools around the country. *"All of these lectures"*, they stated, *"revolve around the diamond engagement ring, and are reaching thousands of girls in their assemblies, classes and informal meetings in our leading educational institutions"*[14].

All in all, it took less than 20 years to convince an entire generation that a well-sized diamond ring was a necessary step in the marriage process. The De Beers marketing machine was now an unstoppable force.

Ayer further began circulating marketing material suggesting, with no point of reference, that a man should spend a month's salary on a diamond ring.

That concept worked so well that De Beers decided to arbitrarily increase the suggestion to two months' salary, which is precisely why people think they need to spend as much on a ring today — because the suppliers of the product made it so. Their infamous poster featured a pouting woman in a scarf, a diamond ring on her finger, and the caption: *"Two months' salary showed the future Mrs. Smith what the future would be like"*[15].

Indeed, it was Ayer who created the 'salary rule' whereby a man should spend a set period of time saving for a diamond engagement ring. But they didn't stop there. N.W. Ayer decided to maximize public exposure to diamonds, hoping to subtly influence their opinion further. They began lending diamond jewelry to Hollywood stars and wrote as guest columnists in newspapers to promote diamonds[16].

It was Mary Frances Gerety, the copywriter, who came up with a slogan you're still familiar with today: "A Diamond Is Forever"[17]. It quickly became the official slogan of De Beers, the most powerful diamond cartel in the world. Ad Age magazine duly awarded "A Diamond is Forever" the best advertising slogan of the 20th century[18].

By the time N.W. Ayer was done, social attitudes had shifted, and diamonds became the norm, rather than the exception. Today, over 80% of women receive diamond rings when they get engaged[19].

With a little bit of help, De Beers successfully brainwashed society into believing that not only were diamonds a rare gem, but you must buy one for the person you love or else you don't love them. An absurd notion, but it worked wonders for them, all while sitting in a room, racking their brains on how to sell diamonds that no one wanted.

It may come as a rude awakening, but the reality is that we covet diamonds for a simple reason: the company that stands to profit from diamond sales decided that we should. Despite diamonds' complete lack of inherent value, we've been sold a manufactured image of diamonds as a status symbol.

We exchange diamond rings as part of the engagement process solely because a diamond company in 1938 decided it would like us to do so. It was purely willed into existence. We buy diamond engagement rings because an advertising agency told us to.

DIAMONDS ARE NOT AN INVESTMENT

As soon as a diamond leaves a jeweler, it loses 50% of its value[20].

For any purchased diamond that remains in its box, unused or unopened, it can be brought to any jewelry store (including the original where it was purchased) for an appraisal. Under no circumstance would the diamond be appraised for anything near what it was just purchased for.

The alarming truth of the matter is that diamonds are a rapidly depreciating asset. They mimic the same declining resale value of a car, laptop, phone or any other mass-produced consumer good. Financial planner, Christopher Cannon, describes it succinctly: *"A diamond ring is not an investment in the sense of making a return on your money, because you will never get what you put in it back out"*[21].

This makes more sense when you compare diamonds to a legitimate investment like gold or silver. The market for gold and silver is extremely liquid and fungible since you can store coins, sell them at any time or even trade them later on. During that time frame, they might even appreciate and provide a hedge against inflation. That is simply not the case with diamonds, however, since the resale market is near illiquid[22]. It explains why the world's largest diamond company had to pay a $10 million fine to the

United States Department of Justice, pleading guilty to colluding with General Electric in price-fixing industrial diamonds[23]. Again, a few years later, they paid a $295 million class-action settlement for price-fixing[24].

Moreover, the non-linear pricing of the different weights of diamonds means that it's not realistic to exchange, for example, two quarter-carats (50 mg) for one half-carat (100 mg). With commodities such as gold, however, it is clear that one 20-gram bar is worth the same as two 10-gram bars, assuming the same purity[25]. There is no universal world price per gram for diamonds. The industry can only look to arbitrary price guides such as the Rapaport Diamond Report, Troy Diamond Report and PriceScope for reference. And hope.

"Investment diamonds are bought for $30,000 a carat," as one New York diamond dealer explains, *"not because any woman wants to wear them on her finger, but because the investor believes they will be worth $50,000 a carat"*[26]. Of course, this is mere delusion. There is no way to resell or flip diamonds for a profit; at least not on this planet. The University of Queensland conducted an international study of whether diamonds were a viable investment alternative to precious metals — especially when protecting investors' wealth during periods of market turmoil[27]. *"Our analysis indicates superior performance by precious metals compared to diamonds"*, they concluded. It was evident for *"investors looking to protect their assets against highly*

volatile market conditions, precious metals remain a better option".

The resale value of diamonds is non-existent. It would appear the memories we attach to our jewelry are what give diamonds significance, not what anyone originally paid for it. And if sentimental value is all we really treasure, we can bypass the notion that it should take the form of glorified graphite.

Ira Weissman, the well-known diamond expert, makes it abundantly clear: *"Diamonds are not an investment — they are a retail product like any other"*[28].

TL;DR

When we consider the overwhelming abundance of diamonds, their decaying resale value along with the fact that, as a society, we've been tricked into coveting them for the past number of decades by an advertising agency, it becomes relatively easy to dismiss diamonds for what they really are: a useless, commonplace mineral.

Diamonds are worthless.

2

MARRIAGE IS TOXIC

Married men live longer than single men. But married men are a lot more willing to die.

— Johnny Carson

What is the point of a marriage?

Romance and relationships are an undeniable part of the human experience. Almost assuredly, most individuals will develop some form of interest by adolescence and continue to pursue companionship well into adulthood.

At some point, we find and fall in love with one particular person — the one we want to live, play and build memories with for the rest of our lives. We remain committed and faithful to each other, for as long as we enjoy one another's warmth and presence.

. . .

That should really be the end of the matter. Yet, for some reason, we have been lead to believe more can (and should) be done. Successful long-term relationships, apparently, must progress to a ceremony of marriage. Why?

For a decision that holds such serious implications on lifestyle, economics and freedom, it is shocking to note most people, when questioned, struggle to provide a reasonable response as to why marriage is a good idea (hint: it's not for the tax incentives).

Indeed, there seems to be no practical benefit to marriage. If anything, it appears to be a detriment to all men who partake in it.

MARRIAGE PROMISES LESS SEX

Access to sex is important to (most of) us. Instinctively, we would assume the institution of marriage is the most fitting way to fulfill this fascination. We would be mistaken. The data is in: sex takes a back seat after couples tie the knot, especially when compared with their cohabitating cohorts.

It is not merely due to a study that followed 2,737 people for six years and found that cohabiters were measurably happier and more confident than married couples[1], or another study which analyzed 1,200 couples to discover married couples gain 6 to 9 pounds more weight than their peers who are single and dating[2]; but perhaps a combination of such factors that lead to a greater frequency of sex among the non-married.

As forensic psychologist Helen Smith (Ph.D.) aptly suggests, couples who cohabitate rather than get married may not be taken for granted as often[3]. This would appear complimentary to the remarks of The Obesity Society's former president Penny Gordon-Larsen (Ph.D.) that when people are still dating, there may be more incentive to stay attractive[4].

Sex matters, and with good reason. A survey conducted by the Pew Research Center showed that a happy "sexual relationship" was the second most important predictor of relational satisfaction ("loyalty" was first), with 70 percent of adults saying it was a "very important" factor[5], even scoring higher than other staples, such as:

- Shared chores
- Adequate income
- Good housing
- Common interests
- Similar religious beliefs
- Agreeable politics

It would seem sex is directly correlated to the health and happiness of our relationships, making it all the more meaningful to note that on any given day, cohabiting young adults are having 13% more sex than their married peers[6]. Perhaps the popular quote, *"Weddings are just funerals with cake"*, has the death in reference to the couple's sex life.

Whether married couples are having sex less as a direct result of marital commitments, financial stress of a mortgage or wedding related debt, lack of physical desire from increased weight gain, monotony, or any other unknown reason, the basic inference would be clear: Avoid marriage if you seek to keep an active and unwavering sex life. While marriage may boast some benefits, as author Susan Squire has noted, *"eroticism is not one of them"*[7].

Our discourse about sexuality in general is dishonest, according to Dan Savage. Known as America's leading sex-advice columnist, he believes it is important to acknowledge the drawbacks of strict arrangements like marriage, which lead to problems such as boredom, despair, lack of variety, sexual death and being taken for granted[8]. There is nothing normative about situations where men sneak out for lap dances, massages and other activity because their wives are no longer interested in sex[9]. It is no surprise to learn the majority of a prostitute's clientage are, of course, married men[10] — they are the most sexually frustrated demographic we can envisage.

It would be horrible to one day find yourself in a sexless marriage, or even among the 15-20% of married couples that have sex fewer than ten times per year[11]. Yet, despite the possibility, men across the world consciously take an enormous risk in opting for marriage, not knowing how they will be impacted in the bedroom. After all, his now wife is the sexual gatekeeper, ultimately deciding the if & when for both of them[12]. To willfully walk into such uncertainty for one of the most important aspects of a successful relationship, you would have to be either foolish or irresponsible; or both.

"*There's a perfectly good reason*", bestselling author Christopher Ryan declares, "*why marriage is often depicted and mourned as the beginning of the end of a man's sexual life*"[13]. Intrinsically, we know it's true.

MARRIAGE FAILURE IS DESTRUCTIVE

40-50% of marriages will end in divorce[14].

69% of the time, it will be initiated by your partner[15], mostly due to some arbitrary level of dissatisfaction[16].

Simply put, the very moment your signature has graced a marriage certificate, you are instantly at a 28-35% risk of imminent danger.

A marriage break-up may not seem too tragic or catastrophic at first glance, but divorce can expose the average person to a world of complications, many of which were never considered or understood from the outset. Beyond the obvious realities of asset dissolution and alimony payments — things that could've been circumvented through prenuptial agreements — divorce leads to the increased likelihood of:

- Anxiety and depression[17]
- Distress[18]
- Poverty[19]
- Drug abuse[20]
- Poor immune function[21]
- Heart failure[22]
- Reduced overall well-being[23]
- Suicide[24]
- Early mortality[25]

Worse yet, the failure of a marriage inflicts considerable damage to society too, more so than we may realize:

Direct and indirect economic consequences of divorce cost the United States $33.3 billion per year[26].

Marital issues like divorce cost American businesses $6.8 billion per year in work loss productivity[27].

Children who are subject to a single parent household commit crime at a much higher rate than those of a two parent home[28].

Perhaps most alarming of all, is that if a friend or family member gets divorced, you are 75% more likely to become divorced also[29]. If it happens to a friend of a friend, your risk of failure is still increased to 33%, creating a ripple effect where married individuals continually expose their loved ones to misfortune through the simple act of association.

As precarious a predicament as this can be, the belief that it won't happen to *you* is perhaps of even greater concern. There is nothing special about your union that makes it immune to the threat of divorce. And yet, as one journalist discovered in interviewing a relatively large sample of individuals whose marriages had ended, every one of them had expected their marriage would last forever[30]. Statistically speaking, your marriage has as much chance of survival as a coin flip.

When we consider there is approximately one divorce occurring every 36 seconds[31], it's almost laughable how much of an idealistic fairytale we've made marriage to be, when it's really just another legal, financial and emotional train wreck waiting to happen. Entire industries exist on the predictable expectancy of divorce. It's a business like any other, lining the pockets of attorneys, judges, motels, pawn shops, liquor stores, storage facilities and others; everyone wins, except you.

On the flip side, if you find yourself among the remaining 50-60% of married couples that does not end up divorced, we must ponder: What was the gain? What advantage can the married claim over their cohabiting/unmarried peers? How many stay married merely out of obligation or fear, as opposed to true happiness? It doesn't take a genius to recognize the risk-to-reward ratio after the fact. Marriage is a high risk effort, with a low yield of return: the type of bet not even a degenerate gambler would entertain.

It's a numbers game. Even on the low end of the divorce spectrum, a 40% failure rate is extremely high. To put that in perspective, ask yourself:

Would you leave your house if there was a 40% chance you would be mugged at some point on your journey?

Would you drive a car if the brakes malfunctioned 40% of the time?

Would you eat a pack of Skittles if 40% of them were poisoned?

. . .

In any context, it is clear and explicit. When it comes to marriage, however, we are either too delusional or ignorant to see that any possible benefit is overshadowed by the looming disaster that is divorce: an affliction on the health, wealth, happiness, safety, security and stability of our communities.

MARRIAGE IS A DREAM KILLER

Many a dream are sacrificed on the altar of marriage.

No one could possibly estimate how many successful businesses, award-winning films, life-changing careers, innovative ideas, real estate projects, world-class inventions, academic prizes and athletic trophies have been stalled, handicapped or deprived of their existence in favor of a legally binding government contract; one that can only be terminated in the presence of large sums of money, lawyers and a judge.

While it may be difficult to accurately attribute a lack of accomplishment to an arrangement like marriage, it seems rather overt when we observe the lifestyles of gleaming historical figures. The most accomplished characters of times past seemed to reach a level of greatness and notoriety from what could be identified as singularity of focus, free from perpetual commitments and taxing obligations. Call it coincidence or direct correlation; marriage wasn't a priority for the zealous individuals who wanted to make a dent in the universe.

Saul of Tarsus, one of the most important figures of the Apostolic Age and a man who wrote several books of the Bible, was such a person. He had one mission: to spread the message of Jesus Christ to the Gentiles[32]. When prompted on the issue of marriage, his instructions were clear:

> *Now to the unmarried and the widows I say: It is good for them to stay unmarried, as I do[33].*

To claim Saul was successful in his main objective may be an understatement. His letters are still observed, analyzed, and revered by billions of people today. His resolve produced a result that has outlasted him for thousands of years.

The same could be said of Jesus Christ himself. From a young boy to the ripe old age of 33, a sole drive directed his steps in a way few could relate to. He was determined, unencumbered, and whether or not he was deity, there is no denying the influence he continues to impose on humanity.

But this concept is not exclusive to religion.

Ted Williams, the left fielder for the Boston Red Sox, could have just as easily fallen into obscurity. His mistress, Evelyn Turner, was very much in love with him, but would only marry Ted under one condition: that she be his number one priority.

His response? *"It's baseball first, fishing second, and you third"*[34].

Who knows what kind of legacy Ted Williams would have carried, had he succumbed to such an ultimatum.

. . .

Nikola Tesla — the consummate inventor, electrical engineer, mechanical engineer and futurist — had expressed his concerns with the idea of marriage. He insisted it would take away from an inventor's work; more specifically:

> *I do not think you can name many great inventions that have been made by married men*[35].

Whether or not his assumption holds water, we can acknowledge the colossal contribution Tesla has made to humanity, arguably only made possible by intentional focus in the absence of marriage.

Orville and Wilbur Wright, the two aviation pioneers credited with inventing, building, and flying the world's first successful motor-operated airplane, also never married. The Wright brothers were too busy making history. As the elder, Wilbur, was known to have asserted:

> *I do not have time for both a wife and an airplane*[36].

Considering he died shortly after making his contribution to humankind, it's safe to say he was indeed correct.

Oprah Winfrey, one of the greatest philanthropists in American history and North America's first black multi-billionaire, also alluded to her success in a similar vein:

> *I think that had Stedman and I gotten married, we certainly wouldn't have stayed married...The show was the true love of my life — it took up all of my energy*[37].

A rather candid admission from the richest African-American of the 20th century.

Yes, the list could go on and on. Notably, it would include the likes of:

- Leonardo Da Vinci
- Ludwig van Beethoven
- Isaac Newton
- Florence Nightingale
- Voltaire
- Jack Daniel
- Henry David Thoreau
- Galileo Galilei
- Herman Melville
- Alexander Graham Bell
- Vincent van Gogh
- Michelangelo
- Edgar Allan Poe
- Andy Warhol
- Alan Turing
- Friedrich Nietzsche
- T. E. Lawrence

It's reasonable to surmise that such individuals would have never reached remarkable levels of dexterity and high distinction, had they decided to settle down. We'd never even know who they were.

A common objection to this suggestion is often the question, "*What about [insert successful person here]? They are extremely accomplished, but they're also married*". This may seem like the correct, knee-jerk response. However, the more sensible question should really be, "*How much further could they have gone?*"

While it's not impossible to be married and still manage to realize your life goals, that doesn't make it a sensible or pragmatic idea. It would be akin to running a marathon with a cannonball chained to your leg: it will slow you down, cause a distraction and introduce compromise in some form or another.

The opportunity cost of marriage is one where our hidden potential goes unfulfilled. Our purpose is stifled, tamed and neutered in exchange for what we perceive to be a better deal. Yet, if we were to imagine any of the aforementioned experts, intellectuals and gifted individuals giving up their talents and skills for a spouse, it would anger and disappoint us all. Not only because it would indirectly reduce our own quality of life, but it would deprive those personalities of true fulfillment — to take away from what they were put on this earth to do.

. . .

Similar to divorce, the pain of such misfortune is not limited to the individual in question. By foregoing our dreams and desires in exchange for marriage, we are robbing the world of our genius. The advancement of mankind remains suspended, until the next generation can pick up the responsibility we left behind.

How much better a state could the world be in at this very moment, had we not been preoccupied with chasing someone of the opposite sex to spend the rest of their lives with us? How many centuries of progress has the human race relinquished in light of seeking attention and gratification from one another?

It's uncomfortable to think about. It's near impossible to answer. But only in asking the question do we begin to understand the loss we are inflicting on humanity. By opting for an archaic institution like marriage, we waive the opportunity to focus on our innate ambitions — the problems we were uniquely born to solve and propel us toward an idealistic future.

TL;DR

It is strangely not surprising to learn that the Spanish word *esposas* simultaneously means both "wives" and "handcuffs". Not many institutions can threaten your sex life, mental & financial well-being, as well as your future hopes and aspirations, the same way an arbitrary piece of paper called "marriage" can. In such an arrangement, only one person has the leverage: and it's not you. Whatever benefit it may have provided in the past, is now irrelevant. It is an outdated union that takes more than it gives.

Marriage is toxic.

3

EMPLOYEES ARE LOSERS

My dad encouraged me to seek a good job with a strong corporation. He didn't understand that, by relying solely on a paycheck from a corporate employer, I would be a docile cow ready for milking.

— Robert Kiyosaki

WHY ARE YOU TOILING FOR SOMEBODY ELSE?

There doesn't seem to be a definitive answer as to why there are more heart attacks on Monday than any other day of the week[1]. The same goes for the origin of the term "Thank God it's Friday", along with its universal popularity.

Be that as it may, it wouldn't be a stretch to imagine our distaste for Monday (and longing for Friday) are tied to our prevailing attitude toward employment. It appears we, as a civilization, dread going to work and ostensibly live for the weekend. We painfully endure the unpleasantries of our job in order to keep our possessions, enjoy our social events and survive long enough for the next paycheck to roll around. It may explain why 64% of employees are not engaged at work; why 14% are "actively disengaged"[2].

The sad part of this predicament, though, is that we have accepted it as a regular part of life. Many of us go our whole lives without questioning the viability of such an arrangement. It would benefit many employers that we continue in not doing so. We don't see that, as employees, we are at a severe disadvantage. We are on the wrong side of the equation.

EMPLOYEES PAY THE MOST TAXES

What's the difference between a tax man and a taxidermist? The taxidermist leaves the skin!

Yes, taxation is evil, unscrupulous, immoral and nefarious. Regardless, we as law-abiding citizens have to carry the burden. And employees bear the brunt of it. The average employee spends 25-35% of their life working to pay taxes. In other words, a few hours of every work day are dedicated exclusively to giving your money away to the government. That's 3-4 months out of every year, which adds up to more than 20 years over your lifetime.

Twenty. Years. That, my friend, is the equivalent prison time for a murder charge. And the sad reality is that employees have no choice but to serve it. Funnily enough, the sentence for tax evasion is only *3 to 5 years!*[3]

Generally speaking, taxes are avoidable. Most people, however, lack the knowledge and resolve to explore the options and strategies available to them. Worse yet, some are convinced we should willingly hand over a portion of our time and money to the government.

As businessman Guy Zanti was once teaching a group of individuals how to play Cashflow 101 (a financial simulation board game) and explaining some of the tax benefits of real estate, a woman in the audience raised her hand:

"Don't you think that it's wrong to reduce your taxes like that?", she asked.

"Isn't it our responsibility to pay the taxes that we owe instead of trying to find ways to steal from the government?"

Guy was stunned. He couldn't believe what he'd just heard[4]. But it's not too crazy to imagine, once you realize that society has been conditioned for compliance — to never question authority, never deviate from the norm and faithfully pay their taxes.

The fact of the matter is that it's *your* money, not the government's. Unless you live in a dictatorship, the money you earn and the wealth you build belongs to you and you alone.

The other reality is that the tax laws, believe it or not, are written to reduce your taxes, not to increase them. Of the 5,800+ pages of tax law, only ~30 are devoted to raising taxes[5]. The remaining pages are devoted entirely to *reducing* your taxes. Explicitly, 99.5% of the tax laws exist solely for the purpose of saving you money.

Unfortunately, you cannot take advantage of the aspects of the law that are there to help you avoid tax if you are an employee. Working for someone else also means you are inadvertently stealing from yourself, your family, and your future.

Why does the government tax employees the most? It's not because they want to punish certain people. It's because they want to reward certain behavior. They incentivize specific activity in order to generate more of it. The government wants the economy to grow. It wants people to invest in energy, agriculture, housing, and job-creating businesses. And it will subsidize these investments accordingly. An employee who contributes to none of these? Not so much.

It's not hard to deduce what needs to be done to benefit from tax breaks. The information is readily available within the tax laws, if you're willing to do the homework. Most people are not. They will spend tons of time and energy to find deals and coupons that save them pennies and dimes, all the while neglecting the tens of thousands of dollars they could be saving by simply doing what the government subsidizes them to.

Owning a business is the classical example. When you own a business, you can change your costs from a personal expense to a business deduction. You can write off expenses for things like your car, travel, food, and education. Further, owning a business allows you to claim depreciation or amortization on the assets that produce income for you. In other words, even though you're profiting from your assets, you still get a tax deduction for them. Yes, the government will pay you to make money and be productive. What employee can do that?

But it's not just business. Income from capital gains, interest, dividends and rentals are taxed at much lower rates than if you were to earn the same money working for somebody else. That's right: Not all income is created equal, with salaries being unquestionably unsavory; they pave the direct path to taxation at the highest rate possible.

It may not seem fair or sensible. Well, it's not meant to be. It just is what it is. With that said, all it takes is some careful planning, research and creativity to join those who are taking advantage of this reality.

Don't complain. Don't try to force those outside the employee bracket to pay their fair share. Instead, become one of those who can legally avoid paying tax by doing what the code incentivizes you to.

EMPLOYEES WILL NEVER BE FREE

As an employee, you're never going to *earn* your way to financial freedom[6].

Nobody drifts into wealth or manages to achieve it due to a lifetime enveloped in the 9 to 5. The numbers just don't work. It's the basic explanation as to why nobody has ever heard of a wealthy taxi driver, office clerk or history teacher. Employees will never experience true freedom. Why? Because they nonchalantly trade 5 days of servitude in exchange for 2 days of freedom, perpetually failing to realize they are in a bad deal.

Would you ever trade $5 for $2? I would assume you answered "No" to that question. And yet, hundreds of millions of us are doing so with a resource much more precious than our money: our time.

Employees voluntarily give up the majority of their week — 71% of it — to an organization in exchange for a relatively small amount of money that is dwindled away on things that won't improve their financial situation, ensuring they will return on Monday to do it all over again. While they're not happy about it, neither are they discontent to the point where they feel the need to take action and actively change their situation.

. . .

It's a plight similar to the howling dog lying on a rusty nail. The story goes like this:

There was a young man walking down the street and happened to see an old man sitting on his porch.

Next to the old man was his dog, who was whining and whimpering. The boy asked the old man, "What's wrong with your dog?"

The old man replied, "He's laying on a nail".

The young man flinched. "Laying on a nail? Why doesn't he get up?"

The old man then replied, "It's not hurting bad enough"[7].

Some may object to the suggestion that their career is a rusty nail that should be done away with. After all, they are working in their desired field; in that "dream job", right?

Wrong. The term "dream job" is an oxymoron. The idea that slaving away for somebody else — making them richer while you sacrifice your youth and freedom — is somehow a dream come true is nothing short of psychotic. The only job you should be dreaming about is the one you decide to pursue out of immense curiosity, excitement, and an insatiable desire to create something worthwhile for yourself.

. . .

There's a reason why a monthly salary is characterized as a harmful addiction much like carbohydrates and heroin[8]. A steady, predictable paycheck becomes a crutch that stunts your growth and keeps you subdued in societal compliance, never questioning your true worth and cutting you off from the deeper, life-fulfilling work you were meant to undertake. The glaring problem with a monthly salary is that we eventually run out of months. Trading time for money is a losing strategy because our time is limited.

On the other hand, conventional wisdom says it is just too risky to leave a stable job in order to venture out on your own and create something you believe the world is in need of. But such wisdom cannot be correct when:

- Jeff Bezos quit his high-paying job on Wall Street to start Amazon.
- Eric Yuan left his VP of engineering job at Cisco to start Zoom.
- Sara Blakely quit her job as a national sales trainer at Danka to start Spanx.
- Rick Wetzel left his job as a brand manager at Nestle to start Wetzel's Pretzels.
- Steve Wozniak resigned from Hewlett-Packard to start Apple with Steve Jobs.

The world is better off with these companies around. They provide jobs for thousands, improve the lives of millions, and the founders & co-founders enjoy freedom we can only dream of. What would have happened, if they bought into the traditional idea of playing it safe with a "normal" job?

The only source of freedom and security in this life resides within us. It won't come from a corporation, the government, or anyone else. Whenever someone espouses that a job is safe and secure, what they don't realize is that security comes at a cost, and the cost is freedom. Living based on security is living based on fear. What you're actually saying is "I'm afraid I won't be able to earn enough based on my skills and determination, so I'll settle for earning just enough to survive or to be comfortable".

Being comfortable is highly overrated. It can make you feel warm and fuzzy, but it won't allow you to grow. To grow as a person, you have to go beyond your comfort zone. You must delve into the uncomfortable. Nobody has ever died of discomfort, but living in the name of comfort has killed more ideas, opportunities, dreams and personal growth than we can ever imagine[9].

As the ultramarathon runner, Dean Karnazes, eloquently describes, *"Western culture has things a little backwards right now. We think that if we had every comfort available to us, we'd be happy. We equate comfort with happiness. And now we're so comfortable we're miserable. There's no struggle in our lives. No sense of adven-*

ture. We get in a car, we get in an elevator, it all comes easy. What I've found is that I'm never more alive than when I'm pushing and I'm in pain, and I'm struggling for high achievement, and in that struggle I think there's magic"[10].

Comfort kills. If your main goal in life is to be comfortable, you will never be wealthy. Moreover, you will never be truly happy. Happiness doesn't stem from relief or contentment. Happiness comes as a result of being in a state of growth and living up to our fullest potential.

The vast majority of people who have achieved freedom have done so with their own business. Whether or not that is right for you is your decision to make, but what is certainly true is the fact that you cannot remain an employee if you desire total freedom.

Your money will always work harder when it's invested; never when it is earned. In other words, there is no amount of hard work you can exert as an employee where you will generate greater wealth than the day before. Your income remains capped and contained, just like your future. Unfortunately, this basic fact goes unnoticed. Billions of people are working extremely hard, yet most of them are still stuck in a set grade of experience with a dictatorship on their income. That's what happens when you opt for the security of a job.

. . .

None of this is to say a job cannot be a means to a freedom-driven end. There is nothing wrong in working a job if merely to serve a temporary goal such as opportunity research, industry networking or startup capital. The vast majority of full-time employees, however, tend to have long-term desires of upper management and climbing the organizational ladder, along with the willingness to make any compromise necessary to get there. It's a losing proposition if there ever was one.

Working for yourself is the way to wealth. Accordingly, there is no shame in pursuing it with all your strength. Those with a fixed mindset may discourage or question such a path, perhaps even quoting archaic aphorisms like *"money cannot buy you happiness"*. They can't seem to understand that:

- Money buys the freedom to watch your kids grow up
- Money buys the freedom to pursue your craziest dreams
- Money buys the freedom to travel anywhere on the planet
- Money buys the freedom to make a difference in the world
- Money buys the freedom to build and strengthen relationships
- Money buys the freedom to do what you love, with financial validation removed from the equation[11]

Money buys freedom.

Will freedom make you happy? Absolutely.

Will you ever be free as an employee? Absolutely not.

EMPLOYEES ARE TRAINED TO RETIRE

Imagine being old, tired, bored, and living on a fixed income — day in, day out — for the rest of your days. It sounds like a slow, painful death. Ironically, this is not far from the truth.

Retirement is nothing more than preparation for the end. In a Harvard study, retirement was shown to be associated with elevated odds of stroke and myocardial infarction (heart attack) onset[12]. Another study found retirement significantly increased the risk of being diagnosed with a chronic condition, particularly, raising the risk of severe cardiovascular disease and cancer. It was also concluded that retirement worsened self-assessed health[13].

A popular study of Kyotango, a small town in Japan with three times more residents over the age of 100 than normal[14], found that the elderly residents followed a routine of what is known as "Ikigai" — the concept of having a direction or purpose in life, providing a sense of fulfillment and meaning[15]. Essentially, it explains why so few residents retire: they find great satisfaction in working. It keeps them happy, and more importantly, alive. There seems to be some truth to the quote, "When you retire, you die".

Working keeps you alive. This theory was supported by a study of 3,000 participants that found employees who continued to work in comparison to those who chose to retire at the same age had a 11% lower risk of all-cause mortality[16]. Another study, where 83,000 adults aged 65+ were examined based on their status of occupation (employed vs. retired) to find that employed older adults had better health outcomes than unemployed older adults, notably in reference to multiple functional limitation[17].

People who are running a company they love, don't retire. People who are happy and enjoying their freedom, don't retire. The only people that are anxious to retire as soon as possible are the ones who don't like what they're doing. The solution, however, would be to change the situation, not to retire.

Unfortunately, the lure of not working, coupled with the opportunity to cash in on the piggy bank that has been slowly filling up for decades, is often too strong to ignore for those who have been indoctrinated to do so from the outset of their career. They do not see any other alternative to the predicament they find themselves in.

Here is where the financial red flags begin to surface. Between the administrative fees, inflation, withdrawal taxes and the opportunity costs of not using those funds for ventures that would have produced far greater returns, the 401(k) is one of the worst financial paths an employee can opt for. But that fact is difficult to accept, especially when you've been informed your funds are tied to the stock market, notified of the employer matching program, and reassured it is actively overseen by an experienced fund manager.

Employees hand over their money to so-called experts, then cross their fingers and hope and pray that everything will turn out well in the end. They fail to take responsibility for their own productivity and worth, replacing the critical values of education and due diligence with misguided faith in financial institutions, corporations and government.

Financial planners habitually convince people that the best thing they can do with their money is to put it away and let it sit for many years and grow on its own "passively", causing them to stop creating value and shirk any intellectual or financial accountability. A 401(k) fundamentally requires an abdication of responsibility. It requires people to stop thinking, to accept social norms and cliches unquestioningly, while allowing external circumstances to dictate their future outlook, all in the name of achieving financial security for the future[18].

But the future is uncertain. It's impossible to predict where we'll be in any number of years, let alone in 30 or 40. All we have is the present moment to maximize our chances in achieving our goals and following the path we truly desire, not to plan and wait for that vision to magically manifest when most of our life has already passed us by. Waiting for retirement to realize a dream is as ridiculous as waiting for the next president to solve all our problems — even if it happens, we wasted our lives in anticipation.

When employees do eventually retire, what do they do when they are completely dependent on their accumulated money? They refuse to utilize it and enjoy it, because their worst fear is that they will lose the "nest egg" they worked so many years to accumulate. It creates a scarcity mentality; a psychology that is fixated on cutting costs and reducing discretionary activity to the point where life is hollow and monotonous, lived at the expense of freedom, joy and productivity.

Tomorrow isn't promised. You could die just a single day before gaining access to the funds you worked decades for. Nothing is guaranteed, including the stockpile you've been contributing to since day one. Meanwhile, your money builds profits for banks, fund managers, and the government who get to keep it and invest it for their own benefit. Ask yourself: Who's the real winner here?

Retirement is a serious physical, psychological and financial risk. It is a well formulated scheme that systematically profits off unsuspecting employees, all the while convincing them of its advantages. Like a herd of cattle, it feeds them only to feed on them.

TL;DR

Employees lose on every front. In pursuit of security, they trade their time and youth, along with any chance of exceptional wealth and genuine happiness. They place their future in the hands of faceless corporations who see them as nothing more than pawns to be exploited. They forfeit the opportunity to create a legacy for their family, only to potentially burden them toward the end with dependency and financial obligation. They don't win in any conceivable scenario.

Employees are losers.

4

SCHOOL IS CHILD ABUSE

Don't confuse schooling with education.

— Elon Musk

IS SCHOOL THE BEST OPTION FOR A CHILD?

Every year, 3-4 million new students decide to make college their logical next step in the pursuit of higher education[1]. Whether by credulity, obligation or ignorance, the factors that went into such a serious determination remain relatively vague.

The legitimacy of school as a whole should be in question.

Why? Maybe because only $0.21 out of every tuition dollar is actually spent on instruction[2]. Or maybe because over the past 25 years, the number of administrators grew twice as fast as the number of students[3].

Or maybe because tuition costs have risen 213% since the 1980s, but wages only rose 67% over the same period[4].

All of the above may explain why 58% of the populace are of the opinion that schools put their own interests ahead of the students who go there[5]. It also contributes to the growing criticism of the entire order, where 78% of younger students no longer believe a four-year degree makes sense[6]. And yet, year after year, millions upon millions of new students flood the school halls like unsuspecting sheep in a slaughterhouse. Either they are being sent against their will, or we are witnessing a classic case of cognitive dissonance. Neither scenario is comforting.

SCHOOL IS A WASTE OF TIME

Not many would disagree with the fact that time is our absolute, most precious resource on this earth as humans.

Ideally, we don't want to squander a minute of it. That is why we grow frustrated with those who waste our time due to their slow driving, unsolicited emails, fluctuating romantic interest, delayed shipping deliveries and late public transportation arrivals (to name just a few examples). Interestingly, it hasn't occurred to us that schooling fritters away more of our time than any other entity ever could.

If we are lucky to live to 100 years old, it's safe to say we deplete 18-25% of our life on schooling alone. Realistically, if we only reach age 75, that number spikes to 24-33%. Think about that: up to a third of your life is expended at school. With massive numbers like that, we should expect a massive return on our priceless investment. Sadly, we both know that not to be true.

School is designed to drag out immeasurably longer than necessary. What could essentially be taught in the space of a few short years, is extended over a prolonged, superfluous period of time. Why? Perhaps the most obvious reason would be in order for institutions to generate the most amount of revenue possible, charging the recurring tuition fee while drip feeding our children just enough to fool us into an assumption of cognitive growth and balanced learning.

What is most alarming, however, is not the fact that school is a waste of time because it provides an education at a shockingly slow rate. It's the fact that it is not providing an education at all.

School, as a collective, has decided to teach its students an irrelevant, ineffectual and impractical curriculum. It is an obsolete training program, serving knowledge which has no connection, no benefit and no value to the outside world. This isn't at all surprising, when we know they teach things like:

- How many rings Saturn has
- When the battle of Hastings was
- How long a snail can sleep for
- How many bones we have
- What the Pythagorean theorem is
- What the capital city of France is
- What paper is made of
- How the water cycle works
- What elements are in the periodic table

The average adult would have forgotten or discarded such random facts shortly after their schooling, precisely because they have no logical or practical use for it. We don't apply the bulk of information we've been instructed to learn, nor would we find ourselves in a situation where we'd ever need to. And yet, children around the country continue to grow up on useless, trivial matters that don't serve them.

It appears that schooling is nothing more than an overpriced childcare facility — keeping kids dumb, derelict and deficient. If the 10,000-hour rule[7] (the idea of becoming an expert through focused effort and deliberate practice over many years) is even remotely true, then we have robbed our children of the very real opportunity of world-class greatness. The chance to explore talents, refine skills and achieve mastery is replaced with shallow exploration of redundant material that deprives a child from a real-world education, hijacking their invaluable time while doing so. It is analogous to the story of the monk and the ferry:

> A monk moved near a river and, wanting to find a way to travel across the water, spent over 10 years forming a type of levitation that would allow him to float across it.
>
> Buddha, who was preaching in town, was confronted by this man, who said to him, "*Look master, look what I have achieved. I can walk across the water!*"
>
> Buddha replied, "*My son, the ferry only costs a nickel*".

A lot of our so-called "learning" is in fact wasted on futile areas that we could have circumnavigated with better tools. It is hard to argue we aren't wasting precious time on school subjects that can be replaced entirely by machines: efficient, precise contraptions that don't get sick, tired, stupid or distracted. Do we really need to learn division & multiplication when we have calculators, cursive handwriting when we have digital devices, or ancient history when we have the internet?

But surely, you might argue, a university degree would not be a waste of time: students have elected a specific subject in order to pursue a meaningful career in it, right? Not so. 73% of people never work in the field they studied for[8]. With the exception of a few occupations, everything else can be learned either on-the-job, or in a fraction of the current time required.

The vast majority of the working population could have bypassed their entire schooling years and be in the same position they are in today. In fact, they would probably be further along in life, due to the added years of work experience and lack of student debt holding them back!

Can you imagine: relinquishing 20-30% of your life — your precious youth — to something that has no tangible benefit whatsoever? Aside from prison, no other institution can deprive someone of their time the way school does. No other institution can do so much irreparable damage, exhausting somebody of a resource which cannot ever be recovered.

SCHOOL BREEDS CONFORMITY

There are 8 learning styles currently known to science[9].

We don't know what percentage of the general population ascribes to which specific learning style. What we do know is that school could not possibly accommodate all of them (at the very least, not effectively). On top of that, it has been discovered the optimal class size has been found to be on the smaller side; up to 15 students[10]. The actual average class size, on last count, is 21[11]. While the data paints a glum picture of the environment our children are confined to, it begs the question: Why is school structured in such a linear fashion, when human beings are unique individuals?

The path paved for students seems rather narrow. If they want to graduate, they have no choice but to abandon their individuality in favor of the scholastic method of doing things, whether that is conducive to their growth or not.

Students aren't seen as autonomous beings as much as common grout. Like a factory assembly line, malleable children are processed through the schooling engine, at scale, to produce copies of the same predetermined mold. The output on the other end is a controlled population that has been conditioned on what to think and how to behave. It is an indoctrination machine.

School breeds conformists: adults who are trained for submission, adhering to societal norms with predictability and full compliance. Self-discovery is actively suppressed. Instead of promoting adventure, experience, solitude, values, apprenticeship and individualism, students are directed into subordination, memorization, standardized testing and uniformity. It is of first concern to have students fit a certain standard, as opposed to leading them in free thought and self-reflection which could prompt an understanding of what it is they truly value and what acts as a catalyst to their personal growth.

Moreover, conformity is damaging to the self-esteem and cognitive well-being of any young mind who finds themselves at odds with what is acceptable and encouraged by the institution. Using a wildlife analogy, it would be tantamount to grading students on the ability to be the best giraffe, despite the classroom being made up of foxes, eagles, elephants, gophers, turtles and tigers; having students instinctively develop the belief they are abnormal, slow or stupid for not being able to "fit in". Rather than embolden and galvanize raw strengths and attributes, school demands students behave as an entirely different species, penalizing those that do not, while rewarding those that do.

. . .

The impressionable nature of children ensures there is little resistance to the standards a school will subject them to. Like a potter's wheel, students can be shaped in any direction desired. Whether it be in bias, belief or opinion, those who control the thoughts of the rising generation, control the future. If there was one thing Adolf Hitler was correct about, it could be his alleged statement, *"He alone who owns the youth, gains the future"*[12]. A similar idea was proposed by Aristotle, who suggested that the first few years of a child's life would determine the rest of their adulthood, professing, *"Give me a child until he is 7 and I will show you the man"*[13]. If true, it solidifies the case against schooling all the more — in the face of inaction, our children will be hardened into a mere shell of their potential and lose their genuine identity to an artificial version of it, based on what an archaic institution has decided it should be.

The president of the Libertas Institute, Connor Boyack, was accurate in his assessment when he noted that children need the ability to explore the world around them in ways that satisfy their curiosity and help them make sense of their world. The freedom to have a say in what they learn, and when and how it's studied, is an empowering gift that will increase a child's sense of independence and excitement in their educational efforts. Coercing them to study during arbitrary times of the day and with mandated assignments, does not provide them the tools and time necessary to learn the things that interest them in the way that suits them best[14].

. . .

All this talk of freedom, control, coercion and institutionalization may seem better suited for a discussion about prison, rather than school. Regrettably, the two are more comparable than we realize. For both institutions:

- Subjects must navigate an authoritarian system
- Emphasis is placed on obedience and order
- A dress code must be followed
- Individual autonomy is largely prohibited
- Scheduled breaks are under constant supervision
- Permission is required to use the restroom
- Input is not allowed for any decision making
- Those who break a rule are swiftly punished
- Individual identity is diminished
- They eat the same meals together at the same time
- Subjects are rewarded for "good" behavior, conditioning them to do what they are told, rather than what they desire

In a nation-wide survey of 21,678 students, 75% of the feelings students reported in their responses to open-ended questions about school were negative: the three most frequently mentioned feelings were "tired", "stressed", and "bored"[15]. The evidence suggests what we already suspect: schooling only caters to a small segment of the population, and actively squeezes the rest into incongruence to the point where we begin to witness survey results as the aforementioned.

. . .

Schools don't really teach anything except how to obey orders[16]. That is the observation of John Taylor Gatto, a schoolteacher who taught in the classroom for nearly 30 years. He concluded schooling had become an education without free will, likening himself to a lid on a container that would prevent children from jumping out to follow their own path[17]. He eventually quit, claiming he *"no longer wanted to hurt kids to make a living"*[18]. The problem is, many still do. Many more know no other way of life.

When an education takes the form of an off-the-shelf, one-size-fits-all package, it is no longer an education; it's borderline brainwashing.

SCHOOL FORESHADOWS FAILURE

There was a striking TV commercial making the rounds several years ago. It conveyed a simple message in the most effective way:

An immaculately dressed young man is casually driving down a residential street, as a voiceover narrator explains what a brilliant and upstanding member of the community he was. *"Jim can solve a Rubik's cube in less than a minute. Jim carries out his neighbors garbage. Jim knows how to ballroom dance"*.

The narrator continues, as Jim pulls into his driveway and parks his car. *"Jim can even recite the name of every president that has ever lived"*. But as Jim exits the vehicle and begins to make his way to the front door, he witnesses the most horrific display of his life.

On the front lawn of his suburban home are his wife and little girl in a hysterical commotion. His daughter has swallowed an awkward object and is struggling to breathe, while his crying, frantic wife is trying everything she can to save her life. Neither parent knows what to do.

Helpless and aghast, Jim can do nothing but watch in despair, as his daughter chokes to death.

"But unfortunately, Jim never did learn the Heimlich maneuver", the narrator notes, as the

commercial fades into black.

The objective of the ad was to encourage viewers to sign up for a promotional first aid course. The words, "Learn What Truly Matters" were the final frame on the screen, along with the company website and telephone number on display. While the ad certainly provoked action, it also provoked the question: Why is one of the most vital subjects in the world, coincidentally, one that is elective?

First aid, evidently, isn't important enough for the school curriculum. Apparently, there are other pressing topics to cover, where the study of dispensing aid to a fellow human is not even an afterthought. How to (potentially) save another life isn't an area we believe our children should have a working knowledge of.

Of course, it doesn't end with first aid. There is a disturbingly vast reservoir of knowledge the public is largely deprived of; the kind of education schools have absolved themselves of teaching. We're referring to critical subject matter, like how to:

- Physically defend yourself
- Analyze risk
- Create a budget
- Make a judgement call
- Invest in stocks and real estate
- Practice proper hygiene

- Interact with others effectively
- Start a campfire
- Think logically and critically
- Balance priorities
- Negotiate for better outcomes
- Maintain healthy relationships
- Ration limited resources
- Build and repair credit
- Understand non-verbal communication
- Hire competent people
- De-escalate a situation
- Set goals for the short & long term
- Change a car tire
- Manage stress, anxiety and anger
- File taxes
- Secure a mortgage
- Prepare for a job interview

Alas, school would rather have us preoccupied with worthless information, ensuring our future be riddled with struggle and hardship instead. Upon their departure from campus, most students are in for a rude awakening when they come to understand how the world actually works, and what society at large truly values.

When 18-year-old Erica Goldson stood at a podium in front of her peers and their parents, she was about to present the most revealing speech a star student could give. Behind her sat the administrators and teachers of the school from which she was graduating. As a school valedictorian, Erica was given the opportunity to speak to her graduating class. Her speech, which by no means was a lengthy one, left the faculty squirming in their seats, as Erica delivered a brutally honest, yet refreshingly authentic and precise account of what had taken place in the years leading up to her fateful address:

> I cannot say that I am any more intelligent than my peers. I can attest that I am only the best at doing what I am told and working the system.
>
> Yet, here I stand, and I am supposed to be proud that I have completed this period of indoctrination. I will leave in the fall to go on to the next phase expected of me, in order to receive a paper document that certifies that I am capable of work. But I contest that I am a human being, a thinker, an adventurer — not a worker. A worker is someone who is trapped within repetition — a slave of the system set up before him.
>
> But now, I have successfully shown that I was the best slave. I did what I was told to the extreme.
>
> While others sat in class and doodled to later become great artists, I sat in class to take notes and become a great test-taker. While others would come to class without their homework done because they were reading about an interest of theirs, I never missed an assignment. While others were creating music and

writing lyrics, I decided to do extra credit, even though I never needed it.

So, I wonder, why did I even want this position? Sure, I earned it, but what will come of it? When I leave educational institutionalism, will I be successful or forever lost? I have no clue about what I want to do with my life; I have no interests because I saw every subject of study as work, and I excelled at every subject just for the purpose of excelling, not learning.

And quite frankly, now I'm scared[19].

Scared! How striking the revelation, that the valedictorian, who is perceived as the most likely to succeed in life, is afraid of what her future holds. As she should be; school has failed her, the same way it has failed millions of others. In fact, being scared might be an understatement for most graduating students; they are leaving school with mounting pressure to find a job as soon as possible, to pay off a debt they cannot even declare bankruptcy to get out of, for a woefully inadequate "education" they have no practical use for. And as far as networking goes, there are superior ways to build a solid Rolodex of contacts without having to take out a legally-binding loan or spend 4 years shackled to trivial and monotonous attendance.

. . .

Students are not prepared for the world on graduation day. The glorification of retention has crippled entire generations. Memorization may *project* the appearance of intellect and indicators of success, but it masks the dangers of ignorance, carelessness & incompetence. When life happens, the regurgitation of information cannot help you. In the midst of tribulation, reiteration of a dissertation cannot save you. Consequently, it is no exaggeration to regard school as the conduit to failure and misfortune.

Undeniably, the futility of school programming, along with the deep-rooted focus on recollection, is damaging to the psychological health of students. But, it doesn't stop there. School is additionally responsible for:

- Negative affects of homework[20]
- Reduced happiness levels[21]
- Prevalence of bullying[22]
- Proliferation of anxiety & depression[23]
- Increased likelihood of alcohol, tobacco, and other illicit drug use[24]

Further, it has created a culture of coddling, where individuals are immobilized and debilitated through incessant sheltering and smothering, leaving them vulnerable and unprepared for reality. In recent years, schools have gone so far as to:

- Host non-competitive sports days where there are "no winners"[25]

- Introduce the concept of "safe spaces" for students who feel marginalized[26]
- Ban and disinvite controversial speakers from appearing on campus[27]
- Change grades after students and parents pressure teachers[28]

The problem with such efforts is that life is indeed competitive on every level. Safe spaces are not practical. Free speech is abundant in a democratic society. And browbeating your way to the top doesn't work. Being exposed to these truths early on can make for a mature individual who may experience a smoother transition into adulthood, as opposed to one who remains continually guarded from all incidents they perceive as stressful, offensive or inconvenient.

There's a saying, "*Prepare the child for the road, not the road for the child*", but these days, president of the Foundation for Individual Rights in Education, Greg Lukianoff, postulates we seem to be doing precisely the opposite. We're trying to clear away anything that might upset children, not realizing that in doing so, we make it far more likely that those children will be unable to cope with such events when they leave our protective umbrella[29]. In a strange twist of irony, the attempt to keep our children safe from harm is what does the most damage; shielding them from adversity never allows for strength, determination or resilience to rise within them. If we send our children to school, we have no one to blame for their failures but ourselves.

TL;DR

The concept of a bona fide educational institution — where students learn skills and subject matter which are explicitly beneficial, succinct, and conducive to the real world — may very well exist. School, of course, fails to meet such criteria. Yes, it may be true that school is just not for *everyone*, but it could also be argued that school is not for *anyone*.

School is child abuse.

5

PASSION IS OVERRATED

Follow your passion? It's probably the worst advice I ever got.

— Mike Rowe

Do we really need passion?

One seemingly universal goal in life is to find or identify a true innate passion; one that will be with us at a young age and never leave our side. For every social media post, fridge magnet and random life tip we are exposed to on a daily basis, there are few more prevalent than those along the lines of what passion is and what it can do for us. Routinely, we are informed:

- Do what you love and you'll never work another day in your life
- The formula for success is just a lot of passion and hard work

- Find your passion and everything else will fall into place

As is common with almost everything else in society, these widespread notions are flawed and misleading at their core. They lack a key understanding of the nature of passion, where it comes from, and how it serves us as human beings.

Undeniably, passion is a strong state that can lead to love, hate, joy, depression, creativity, addiction and many other emotions on either side of the spectrum. What's most compelling, however, is that for the most part, passion is not nearly as important as we once thought.

PASSION IS CREATED

Dirty Jobs was a television series on the Discovery channel that showcased strange, disgusting and messy occupational duties. The star of the show was also the host; an everyday man named Mike Rowe. He would, as he describes, be an apprentice for all kinds of jobs, where he gives an honest account of what it's like to be these workers for one day in their life.

With over 170 shows spanning 9 seasons, it gained a great deal of fame and notoriety. People began to see Mike Rowe as somewhat of an expert in the realm of employment, vocation training and career guidance. Having worked in almost every industry imaginable, it was not surprising to see why.

One ordinary day, a fan of the show wrote in the following:

> Hey Mike!
>
> I've spent this last year trying to figure out the right career for myself and I still can't figure out what to do. I have always been a hands-on kind of guy and a go-getter. I could never be an office worker. I need change, excitement, and adventure in my life, but where the pay is steady. I grew up in construction and my first job was a restoration project. I love everything outdoors. I play music for extra money.

I like trying pretty much everything, but get bored very easily. I want a career that will always keep me happy, but can allow me to have a family and get some time to travel. I figure if anyone knows jobs it's you so I was wondering your thoughts on this if you ever get the time! Thank you!

— Parker Hall

Mike Rowe, with all his wit and experience, took the time to reply with the following:

Hi Parker,

My first thought is that you should learn to weld and move to North Dakota. The opportunities are enormous, and as a 'hands-on go-getter,' you're qualified for the work. But after reading your post a second time, it occurs to me that your qualifications are not the reason you can't find the career you want.

I had drinks last night with a woman I know. Let's call her Claire. Claire just turned 42. She's cute, smart, and successful. She's frustrated though, because she can't find a man. I listened all evening about how difficult her search has been. About how all the 'good ones' were taken. About how her other friends had found their soulmates, and how it wasn't fair that she had not.

'Look at me,' she said. 'I take care of myself. I've put myself out there. Why is this so hard?'

'How about that guy at the end of the bar,' I said. 'He keeps looking at you.'

'Not my type.'

'Really? How do you know?'

'I just know.'

'Have you tried a dating site?' I asked.

'Are you kidding? I would never date someone I met online!'

'Alright. How about a change of scene? Your company has offices all over – maybe try living in another city?'

'What? Leave San Francisco? Never!'

'How about the other side of town? You know, mix it up a little. Visit different places. New museums, new bars, new theaters...?'

She looked at me like I had two heads. 'Why the hell would I do that?'

Here's the thing, Parker. Claire doesn't really want a man. She wants the 'right' man. She wants a soul-mate. Specifically, a soul-mate from her zip code. She assembled this guy in her mind years ago, and now, dammit, she's tired of waiting!!

I didn't tell her this, because Claire has the capacity for sudden violence. But it's true. She complains about being alone, even though her rules have more or less guaranteed she'll stay that way. She has built a wall between herself and her goal. A wall made of conditions and expectations. Is it possible that you've built a similar wall?

Consider your own words. You don't want a career — you want the 'right' career. You need 'excitement' and 'adventure,' but not at the expense of stability. You want lots of 'change' and the 'freedom to travel,' but you need the certainty of 'steady pay.' You talk about being 'easily bored' as though boredom is out of your control. It isn't. Boredom is a choice. Like tardiness. Or interrupting.

It's one thing to 'love the outdoors,' but you take it a step further. You vow to 'never' take an office job. You talk about the needs of your family, even though that family doesn't exist. And finally, you say the career you describe must 'always' make you 'happy.'

These are my thoughts. You may choose to ignore them and I wouldn't blame you — especially after being compared to a 42-year-old woman who can't find love. But since you asked...

Stop looking for the 'right' career, and start looking for a job. Any job. Forget about what you like. Focus on what's available. Get yourself hired. Show up early. Stay late. Volunteer for the scut work. Become indispensable. You can always quit later, and be no worse off than you are today. But don't waste another year looking for a career that doesn't exist. And most of all, stop worrying about your happiness. Happiness does not come from a job. It comes from knowing what you truly value, and behaving in a way that's consistent with those beliefs.

Many people today resent the suggestion that they're in charge of the way the feel. But trust me, Parker. Those people are mistaken. That was a big lesson from Dirty Jobs, and I learned it several hundred times before it stuck. What you do, who you're with, and how you feel about the world around you, is completely up to you.

Good luck,

— Mike

P.S. I'm serious about welding and North Dakota. Those guys are writing their own ticket.

P.P.S. Think I should forward this to Claire?[1]

The inquisitor wanted a simple answer to what career they should pick. The response, essentially, was that there is no way to know — not until you try a few things first — taking the first step in any one direction, is infinitely better than remaining idle in constant reflection of your options. Exposing yourself to the workforce in any capacity is greater than shying away from it until a seemingly opportune moment presents itself. Trying many different jobs and trusting yourself to gradually understand what it is you want to commit to, is likely the most appropriate answer to the question at hand.

Perhaps the great Mike Rowe understood that the purpose and satisfaction you may typically find in *one* specific career can be realized in *any*. His response seems to express the following sentiment: *Work in many different industries. Learn a lot of new things. You will eventually develop a passion for one of them. Follow that path.*

Alas, our distorted view of passion is what makes this advice difficult to follow. We assume passion is either assigned at birth and buried deep in our subconscious, or something just "out there" we find by luck or happenstance. Neither are true.

Passion isn't some sacred object that is lost or misplaced, where you must venture to find it. More often than not, it is something to be shaped and nurtured. Most don't know what their genuine passions are — estimates hovering around the 80% mark[2] — and unfortunately, they probably never will; simply because they won't try enough things. It's not surprising to comprehend, since we humans are not inclined to veer outside our comfort zone to explore unfamiliar territory, no matter how rewarding the adventure may be. We settle for options that are near and tolerable, rather than forge the path of self-actualization. The lure of stability overrides our desire for absolute clarity.

Coaches and consultants often advocate for a prevailing thought experiment, where a person is advised to list a number of their perceived interests, followed by the ensuing task of identifying which of these could practically lead to a sustainable business or career. But this is problematic. Interests are not discovered through introspection. Interests are triggered by interactions with the outside world[3]. As chair of psychology at UCLA, Robert Bjork, purportedly claimed, *"One real encounter, even for a few seconds, is far more useful than several hundred observations"*[4].

Bjork's statement echoes the conclusion made by psychologist Henry Roediger at Washington University, where he had students divided into separate subject groups to study certain texts. One group studied for 4 sessions. Another group studied only once, but was tested 3 times. In future examination, the group that was tested would score 50% higher than the group who had only studied. Despite studying one-fourth as much, they had learned far more[5]. Trial and error transcended theory. It complements what entrepreneur Marie Forleo has affirmed, that, *"Clarity comes from engagement, not thought"*[6].

When researcher in the psychology of music, John Sloboda, conducted a study at a British boarding school, he was surprised to find that the exceptional music students were those who came from less musically active families, and that the "sheer amount of lessons or practice time" was not a good indicator of exceptionality. Remarkably, the best students were those who explored multiple instruments. Nearly all of the more accomplished students had played at least three instruments, proportionally much more than the lower-level students. More than half played four or five[7].

Psychologists have highlighted this "sampling period" as the most common indicator of prospective excellence. Sports scientist, Ross Tucker, makes a similar observation, declaring, *"We know that early sampling is key, as is diversity"*[8]. Experimenting with various disciplines and special interests is critical in manufacturing passions which stand the test of time.

What does this sampling period look like? Pragmatically, no one could tell you. There is no script, playbook or template to follow. Like a blank slate — a "Tabula rasa" state — this is a journey with no map or master plan. It's a mountain you must climb on your own. *"If you can see your path laid out in front of you step by step, you know it's not your path,"* Joseph Campbell once said. *"Your own path you make with every step you take. That's why it's your path"*[9]. Where you make the first move is not merely as important as the act of making it. The only way to fail is to recede back into comfort and familiarity, convincing yourself that you are already passionate about what you currently do.

. . .

Yes, you may enjoy some aspects of selling insurance, completing deliveries or servicing irate customers. Yet, it is more than reasonable to assume there is something else you can be much, much, much more passionate about. We all can. Even those who claim to be happy and satisfied are probably not doing what they are truly passionate about. Not out of ignorance, or incompetence, or negligence; but out of convenience. Settling for less-than-ideal outcomes is a recurring theme in human history. But it doesn't have to be for those who desire more.

This isn't about choosing between good and bad. It's about choosing between better and best. And that's not an easy thing to do. As psychology professor Barry Schwartz correctly noted, *"Learning to choose is hard. Learning to choose well is harder. And learning to choose well in a world of unlimited possibilities is harder still"*[10]. It is also mightily worth pursuing. As someone who has worked 40+ jobs in 20+ industries over a 20+ year period, I can tell you that passion is developed, not discovered. Identifying it from study or intuition is near impossible. It is cultivated; refined in an environment of curiosity, humility and active exploration.

You don't find your passion. You create it.

PASSION FOLLOWS COMPETENCE

Most of us may be familiar with the satirical, office humor comic strip known as Dilbert. It was a roaring success in the 1990s, spawning dozens of books, an animated television series, a video game, and hundreds of Dilbert-themed merchandise items. What we may not know is the story behind the creator, Scott Adams. Dilbert was certainly not Scott's first venture or idea. He tried a number of other businesses that ultimately failed. What was interesting about his story, however, was how he describes the ebb-and-flow of his passions. In his own words:

> I've been involved in several dozen business ventures over the course of my life, and each one made me excited at the start. You might even call it passion. The ones that didn't work out — and that would be most of them — slowly drained my passion as they failed. The few that worked became more exciting as they succeeded.
>
> For example, when I invested in a restaurant with an operating partner, my passion was sky-high. And on day one, when there was a line of customers down the block, I was even more passionate. In later years, as the business got pummeled, my passion evolved into frustration and annoyance. The passion disappeared.
>
> On the other hand, Dilbert started out as just one of many get-rich schemes I was willing to try. When it started to look as if it might be a

> success, my passion for cartooning increased because I realized it could be my golden ticket. In hindsight, it looks as if the projects I was most passionate about were also the ones that worked. But objectively, my passion level moved with my success. Success caused passion more than passion caused success[11].

Successful people are interviewed frequently. You can find such recorded segments on television programs, social media channels, radio stations and podcasts ad nauseam. At some point during any such conversation, they are almost certainly asked to provide a nugget of wisdom or insight for the audience of listeners. Habitually, they give cliche responses, like "chase your passion" or "work hard on things you enjoy doing". These answers may be acceptable, but they are also probably not true. Perhaps, like Scott Adams, their competence, perseverance and risk tolerance is actually what lead to their success, with an influx of passion coming in at the tail end of the equation — a byproduct of their achievement, not a requisite.

Passion appears further along the path, not at the beginning. Passion follows mastery, not the other way around. It is only when we get really good at something that we develop a passion that is sustainable over a long period of time[12]. Wanting the passion first before putting in the work is like wanting to get paid before you begin a job[13]. It's completely backward thinking, and yet, 78% of people hold this "fit mindset", where they believe it is ideal to find an activity or job about which they are immediately passionate; something that feels intuitively right from the get-go[14]. Individuals who adopt this attitude for passion tend to overemphasize their initial feelings. They are more likely to choose pursuits based on preliminary assessments, not potential for growth — even though the latter is generally more important for lasting fulfillment and satisfaction[15]. It goes without saying, such an approach can bring about real problems over the course of a lifetime.

The solution to this dilemma seems clear: invariably stick with one discipline long enough to develop skill and expertise, which will instinctively induce passion for it. But would this theory work for *every* individual? For *every* kind of activity?

One man put it to the test. László Polgár, a Hungarian educational psychologist, formed the view in the 1960s that great performers are made, not born. His research persuaded him that the greatest performers had all been made to focus and work on their field of eventual achievement from an early age, and he believed he understood the process well enough that he could make it happen himself. He publicly asked for a woman who would marry him, have children with him, and help him conduct the experiment. Amazingly enough, he found such a woman, a Hungarian-speaking schoolteacher in the Ukraine named Klara. László and Klara had 3 daughters —

Susan, Sophia and Judit. When they were old enough, the experiments began.

László was so sure his training program would work for any area that he wasn't picky about which particular one he and Klara would target, and the two of them discussed various options. Languages were one option: Just how many languages might it be possible to teach a child? Mathematics was another possibility. Top-flight mathematicians were highly regarded in Eastern Europe at the time, as the Communist regimes sought ways to prove their superiority over the decadent West. Eventually, he and Klara settled on a third option. "We chose chess. Chess is very objective and easy to measure", Klara would later tell a newspaper reporter.

It didn't take long for the Polgárs' experiment to bear fruit. Susan, the firstborn, was just 4 years old when she won her first tournament with 10 wins, 0 losses, and 0 ties. At age 15, she became the top-ranked woman chess player in the world, and she went on to become the first woman to be awarded grandmaster status via the same path that the males must take. Sofia, the second daughter, also had an amazing chess career.

Judit, however, was the crown jewel of László Polgár's experiment. She became a grandmaster at 15 years, 5 months, making her at that time the youngest person, male or female, to ever reach that level. She was the #1 ranked women's chess player in the world for 25 years, until she eventually retired from the sport[16]. Would you suppose Judit Polgár was passionate about the sport she was so great at? Well, she left no room for speculation: *"I cannot live without chess. It is an integral part of my life. I enjoy the game!"*[17].

The Polgár story vividly illustrates how passion can be fabricated in *any* person, for *any* endeavor. There is no other logical explanation for how all three children became world-class players in an ancestrally foreign sport that is historically male dominated: all while forming a significant degree of interest in it.

Whether it's comic illustration, politics, business, fitness, chess or any other pursuit; the evidence is undeniable. We can choose what we are passionate about. Rather than being fooled by fascination, we need only follow the straight line of proficiency; passion seeking us out along the way.

PASSION IS NOT ENOUGH

There are many positive aspects of passion; laudable things like motivation, clarity, energy, intensity, happiness and fulfillment (to name a few). Be that as it may, it lacks the necessary and practical components for lasting performance.

Passion is not the missing ingredient to success. In fact, sometimes, passion can act as an impediment, threading an inadvertent web of delusion and failure, entangling even the best of us. As this loan officer explains:

> When I worked for a large bank in San Francisco, my boss taught us that you should never make a loan to someone who is following his passion. For example, you don't want to give money to a sports enthusiast who is starting a sports store to pursue his passion for all things sporty. That guy is a bad bet, passion and all. He's in business for the wrong reason.
>
> My boss, who had been a commercial lender for over 30 years, said the best loan customer is one who has no passion whatsoever, just a desire to work hard at something that looks good on a spreadsheet. Maybe the loan customer wants to start a dry-cleaning store or invest in a fast-food franchise — boring stuff. That's the person you bet on. You want the grinder, not the guy who loves his job[18].

For every passionate winner, there are millions of passionate losers, which leaves us to wonder what alternate factor might be at play here. If the winning ticket is not due to raging passion, would it be attributed to something else, say, the genetic gifts & natural talents we possess?

Many studies of accomplished individuals have tried to figure out the key elements of their achievements. Yet over and over again, when researchers have looked at large numbers of high achievers, at least in certain fields, most of the people who became successful in their field did not show early evidence of gifts. Similar findings have turned up in studies of musicians, tennis players, artists, swimmers, and mathematicians. Such findings do not prove that talent doesn't exist. But they suggest an intriguing possibility: that if it does, it may be irrelevant[19].

Talent is much less important than we usually think. They don't seem to play the crucial role that we generally assign to them, and it's far from clear what role they do play. Indeed, if some sort of innate ability were playing a role in determining who rose to the top of their field, it would be much easier to spot these individuals far earlier on in their career — something that nobody has ever been able to consistently do.

. . .

Cal Ripken Sr., manager and coach of the Baltimore Orioles, makes a similar observation: *"I saw a lot of guys come through the minor leagues who were blessed with all the ability that you'd want to be blessed with, but...they didn't make it to the big leagues. I saw some other guys come through the minor leagues who didn't have half the talent that some of these other people had, but...they wound up going to the big leagues"*[20].

So, if success is not rooted in gifts and talent, surely it must be connected to training and experience?

It is often assumed that someone who has been driving for 20 years must be a better driver than someone who has been driving for 5; a doctor who has been practicing medicine for 20 years must be better than one who has been practicing for 5; a teacher who has been teaching for 20 years must be better than one who has been teaching for 5. But no. Research has shown that, generally speaking, once a person reaches that level of "acceptable" performance and automaticity, the additional years of "practice" don't lead to improvement. If anything, the doctor, teacher or driver who's been at it for 20 years is likely to be a bit worse than the one who's been doing it for only 5, and the reason is that these automated abilities gradually deteriorate in the absence of deliberate efforts to improve[21].

Research on many specialties shows that doctors who have been in practice for 20 or 30 years do worse on certain objective measures of performance than those who are just 2 or 3 years out of medical school. It turns out that most of what doctors do in their day-to-day practice does nothing to improve or even maintain their abilities[22]. And only two out of sixty-two studies have shown doctors to have gotten better with experience[23].

We see this occurrence quite often. Seasoned stockbrokers fail to apply logical thinking skills and rational decision-making practices at the same rate as ordinary traders[24]. Wine experts have been found to be no better at functioning domain-specific expertise than their novice counterparts[25]. Licensed psychiatrists and psychologists seem to be no more effective at performing therapy than laypeople who've received minimal training[26].

Contrary to expectations, training and experience is no indication of ideal performance or long-term preeminence in any one area. If anything, it should give pause the next time you hear somebody pass off their years of experience as rationale or reassurance. Excellence, therefore, is not the result of intensive training, lifelong experience, genetic gifts nor natural talents; and certainly not the aftermath of burning passions. Where, then, does the answer lie?

Deliberate practice. That's where.

At first, it may just sound like another term for "repetition" or "preparation", however, it has its unique distinction. Deliberate practice is about struggling in certain targeted ways — operating at the edges of your ability, where you make mistakes — experiences where you're forced to slow down, make errors, and correct them[27].

Deliberate practice is not the equivalent of doing the same thing over and over again mindlessly; that is merely a recipe for stagnation and gradual decline. The purpose of the repetition is to understand where your weaknesses are and focus on getting better in those areas, sampling different methods for improvement until you discover something that works.

Passion falls short in the wake of what deliberate practice can offer. Namely, a neural insulator called "myelin".

Every human skill, whether it's drawing cartoon characters or kicking a soccer ball, is created by chains of nerve fibers carrying a tiny electrical impulse. The role of myelin is to wrap those nerve fibers the same way that rubber insulation wraps a copper wire, making the signal stronger and faster by protecting the circuits from interruption. When we fire the intended impulses over and over — with deliberate practice — our myelin responds by wrapping layers around that neural circuit, each new layer adding a little more dexterity. The thicker the myelin gets, the better it insulates; the faster and more accurate our movements and thoughts become[28].

There is, biologically speaking, no substitute for such attentive repetition. Nothing you can do — declaring, visualizing, studying, meditating — is more effective in building skill than executing the action, firing the impulse down the nerve fiber, fixing errors, honing the circuit[29].

Myelination is a slow process. Building up myelin over years of acute signals through nerve fibers may seem like a daunting task. Yet on the contrary, knowledge of this phenomenon and how it works can serve to increase patience and persistence along the road of adversity and frustration. Like a map of your desired destination, understanding where you are and what direction you need to follow is a surefire way to arrive at your goal much sooner, than to pick any random path and hope for the best (which most do).

Myelin is the great equalizer. No longer do we need to accept the false, paralyzing narrative that performance and success is reserved for the gifted, the talented, the trained or the passionate. It is available to you and to everyone.

Passion isn't the key to success. Myelin is.

TL;DR

The malleable, erratic and arbitrary nature of passion make it an improper goal to pursue. And while it can serve as a source of motivation and encouragement when realized, it falls short over the long-term as inconsistent and unsustainable in the face of alternative, preferential factors; its presence bearing no indication of looming success.

Passion is overrated.

6

CHARITY IS PERVERSE

It makes me feel good to use my training in economics to "save" poor people. And in the process, I reduce them to objects that I use to fulfill my own need to accomplish something.

— Steve Corbett

WHO IS CHARITY ACTUALLY HELPING?

There are over 1.5 million charities in the U.S., with thousands of new ones established each year[1]. While they vary in cause and objective, they have the shared goal of making the world a better, safer, healthier, happier place. They seek to solve society's biggest problems; issues like homelessness, famine and poverty. With so many organizations at the helm battling destitution on a daily basis, questions instinctively arise, like: What has been their impact? How much further do we have to go? And how many more charities would we really need in order to solve the issue, once and for all?

The answer is not as simple as once thought. In fact, the question may need to be flipped: How many charities can we do away with and see the exact same results we do now?

Most likely all of them. We have been combating poverty for many decades, and poverty won. Regardless, we still believe one day, maybe, we can donate enough money and resources to the poor and finally tap poverty into submission. How utopian!

The idea that charity can expunge poverty is a fantasy. If anything, charity makes things worse; far worse. It is, as Karl Kraus describes of psychoanalysis, *"the disease it purports to cure"*[2].

Rather than alleviate, charity exacerbates. It stands in the way of growth and transformation. It is a humanitarian disaster. It isn't just part of the problem — it *is* the problem.

CHARITY CREATES DEPENDENCE

Sending food to Somalia. Digging wells in Tanzania. Donating clothes to the local homeless shelter. These all seem like such commendable works; no one would dare question or criticize us for them. But what may come as a surprise is, those closest to the ground — the ones who are on the receiving end of this constant outpouring of generosity — would quietly admit that it may actually be hurting them, rather than helping.

How? Dependency. In the most simple terms: When we supply the impoverished with everything they need, we disempower them. We destroy their incentive. We leave them dependent on us.

Subsidizing non-productivity hurts the poor. Undoubtedly, our intentions are pure: help the underprivileged find their feet and become productive members of society. Unfortunately, our desired result is everted entirely.

We've all probably heard the adage: feed a man fish and he'll eat for a day; teach a man to fish and he'll eat for a lifetime. While we tend to agree with the notion, we betray it in everyday life. From handing the homeless person a dollar, to large scale food pantries and soup kitchens — our actions palpably foster dependence. In an attempt to combat the immediate crisis of hunger, we continue to feed a man a fish to their own detriment.

. . .

One church experienced this firsthand. Collectively deciding to address poverty via giving, they began purchasing Christmas presents for children in the local housing projects. Church members went door to door, singing Christmas carols and delivering wrapped toys to the children in each apartment. Although it was awkward at first, members of the church were moved by the big smiles on the children's faces and were encouraged by the warm reception of the mothers. In fact, the congregation felt so good about the joy they had brought, they decided to expand the ministry into baskets of candy at Easter and turkeys at Thanksgiving.

Alas, after a number of years, the lead pastor noticed he was struggling to find enough volunteers to deliver gifts. At the congregational meeting, he asked the members why their enthusiasm was waning, but it was difficult to get a clear answer. Finally, one member spoke up: "*Pastor, we are tired of trying to help these people out. We have been bringing them things for several years now, but their situation never improves. They just sit there in the same situation, year in and year out*"[3].

It would certainly be frustrating to donate to a single cause over an extended period of time, only to witness limited progress (if any at all). Resentment toward the destitute may form, as we attribute their predicament to their own lack of desire to improve their situation. Ironically, it is *our* incessant yearning to help that leaves the needy in a state of helplessness. Our free distribution of resources produces ever-growing handout lines, diminishing the dignity of the poverty-stricken, while only increasing their dependency.

Another church group decided to devote efforts internationally, in a remote Honduran village. On the initial visit, one need became obvious: water. The village women had to carry water from a supply source miles away, spending hours each day trudging in the oppressive heat. It seemed self-evident that a water well would solve many problems for the community. The church had connections with well-drilling engineers, along with funds to cover the costs. And since this was a desperate need that could be addressed directly, the church immediately commenced a well-digging initiative.

When the first water was pumped to the surface and villagers filled their jugs with cool, pure water, there was a great celebration. There were cheers, hugs of joy, and many "gracias, señors". They had literally changed these people's lives.

The following year, however, as the church's returning missioners rumbled up the dusty road toward the village, they observed women carrying water jugs as they had done before. Arriving at the village, the team saw that the well was idle. The pump had broken down, and there was no way to draw precious water to the surface. The ministry team knew what to do; they repaired the pump. Soon, water was flowing in the village once more.

By the time the team returned the following year, the pump had broken down yet again, and women had resumed their toilsome treks. This happened year after year; The villagers would simply wait until their benefactors returned to fix their well for them[4].

Another nonprofit organization, wanting to assist a village in Colombia with its rice production, gathered the villagers into a cooperative and bought them a thresher, a motorized huller, a generator, and a tractor. Rice production boomed, and the cooperative sold the rice at the highest price the farmers had ever received. The project appeared to be a tremendous success. The nonprofit organization then left the village.

Several years later, one of its staff members returned to the village, only to find that the cooperative had completely disbanded and that all of the equipment was broken down and rusting away in the fields. In fact, some of the equipment had never been used at all. Yet, as the staff member walked through the village, the people pleaded with him, "If your team would just come help us again, we could do so much!"[5].

As free resources continue to flood in, the catalyst for change will continue to decline. People become conditioned to wait on the next mission group for deliverance, rather than take their destiny into their own hands and build their own future. Dignity is eroded as people come to view themselves as charity cases for wealthy visitors, how they pose with smiling faces for pictures to be used in marketing material to attract the next wave of donors. As one social worker from Nicaragua had wistfully concluded, *"They are turning my people into beggars"*[6].

In our naiveté and prevalent ignorance, we observe the plight of the poor as a simple problem that would go away if we just threw more money at it. Optimistically, we perceive our monetary contributions as analogous to a pair of crutches — assistance for the purposes of gradual restoration and wholeness — yet, such giving is more similar to a wheelchair: a faux solution that doesn't solve anything, ensuring the problem never goes away.

Give once, it elicits appreciation.

Give twice, it creates anticipation.

Give thrice, it establishes expectation.

The downward spiral of dependency begins with innocent acts of charity. It may feel good. It may convince us we are making a positive difference in the world. On the contrary; they are fleeting, counter-productive and covertly harmful acts indeed.

CHARITY UNDERMINES COMMUNITIES

Let's be honest. We don't take part in the global effort to eradicate poverty because it's the virtuous and moral thing to do. While a noble thought, it just isn't our primary motive (if one at all). The only reason we really care about sacrificing our time and effort for those less fortunate, is because charity is good for *us*. The satisfaction we derive from clothing, feeding, teaching, healing and housing our fellow human-in-need is hard to top.

With self-gratification as the prime mover, it's no surprise to find several relief, rehabilitation or development resolutions running at complete odds with what is actually beneficial for those in the thick of the chaos. Instead of an education, we give them socks. Instead of a job, we hand them soap. We assume we fully grasp the underlying factors affecting the afflicted; we think we know better than the local paupers. Fundamentally, we demonstrate a crass case of paternalism.

Folks on mission trips tend to exhibit a messiah complex, persuaded they are a long-awaited gift to the communities they're temporarily visiting. They are unaware how many times the natives have seen this tired movie play out. And as much knowledge as humanitarian workers may possess concerning things like how to plant crops, cook food, manage hygiene, or cure diseases, it is narrow-minded to infer the materially deprived have nothing to offer on such matters. If anything, do-gooders could absorb as much as they impart.

We seem to forget: the poor constantly face tribulations we have little-to-no understanding of. Only those dwelling in such conditions can determine what they are most in need of; much more than an outsider ever could. To dismiss these details in lieu of a "we know what's best for you" approach is to display a severe lack of empathy, voiding the very essence of charity we would aspire to espouse.

It's equally belittling to simply copy what works elsewhere. Attempting to apply insights from one culture and framework to the next is a misguided means of assistance. Success in one context does not mirror in another; it could very well prove the opposite. The fact that someone has created a strong agricultural business in the neighborhoods of Montevideo, for example, does not mean they are able to reproduce results for an apricot farmer in the mountainous settings of rural Armenia. Every problem has nuance, and deserves the patience and willingness to discover the most appropriate solution. To think otherwise is to deride the individuality and unique circumstances of the misfortunate, lumping them together as indistinguishable riffraff.

Whether out of pity, indifference or paternalism, when we give to the needy, we are unlikely to see them as social equals. French philosopher and theologian, Jacques Ellul, came to a similar conclusion, claiming, *"Almsgiving is Mammon's perversion of giving. It affirms the superiority of the giver, who thus gains a point on the recipient, binds him, demands gratitude, humiliates him and reduces him to a lower state than he had before"*[7]. They become a lesser species we feel obliged to care for, rather than fellow humans we can rebuild with.

Charity undermines the very beings it seeks to uplift. Charity encourages the dehumanization of the poor, facilitating our hubris and superiority over them. In doing so, it opens the door to widespread economic damage through our reckless acts of empty generosity.

In 1998, when Hurricane Mitch devastated Central America, U.S. mission teams rushed to Honduras to help rebuild homes destroyed. On average, they spent approximately $30,000 per home; homes that locals could have built for only $3,000 each. The money spent by one campus ministry for their Central American mission trip to repaint an orphanage would have been sufficient to hire 2 local painters, 2 full-time teachers and purchase new uniforms for every student in the school[8].

A mosquito net maker in Africa manufactures around 500 nets a week. He employs ten people, who (as with many African countries) each have to support upwards of 15 relatives. However hard they work, they can't make enough nets to combat the malaria-carrying mosquito. Enter the vociferous Hollywood movie star, who rallies the masses, and goads Western governments to collect and donate 100,000 mosquito nets to the afflicted region at a cost of a million dollars. The nets arrive, the nets are distributed, and a "good" deed is done. With the market flooded with foreign nets, however, the mosquito net maker is promptly put out of business. His ten workers can no longer support their 150 dependents (who are now forced to depend on handouts), unintentionally crippling whatever slim chance for sustainable development there may have been[9].

After an eye-opening trip to Argentina, Blake Mycoskie returned home to create a shoe company with a mission. His concept was slightly different to the traditional business model: for every pair of shoes sold, he would donate a pair to a child in need; he'd been persuaded that lack of shoes were a major contributor to diseases in children. As the story goes, the one-for-one concept took off rather quickly, with TOMS shoes selling over 10,000 pairs in its first year, helping thousands of needy children while also inspiring a new category of commerce. But despite its initial success, sustainability of the model has been called into question. One entrepreneur described the charity angle as "awkward, feel-good publicity that had no lasting economic benefit". Understandably so — giveaway programs undercut small businesses trying to make a living on local production. Used clothing imports caused a 50% increase in unemployment in the African textile industry from 1981 to 2000.

And from 1992 to 2006, half a million workers in Nigeria lost their jobs due to the inflow of donated clothing[10].

By flooding the market with suitcases full of free stuff, everybody loses. Beyond the economic tragedy of business closures and bankruptcy, individuals are unjustly disheartened of their ambition and self-assurance. Very few people desire a life of laziness and passivity — they want to make something of their lives! According to the World Values Survey, the number of people who believe that it is "humiliating to receive money without having to work for it" is comparable across the globe, irrespective of socioeconomic status[11]. Many derive immense pride from the ability to provide for themselves, and try to avoid making use of programs like food stamps in part for that reason. Similarly, an inability to provide for themselves leads to strong feelings of inadequacy among many welfare recipients[12].

It wouldn't be a stretch to say our charity does more harm than good. Truly, it could be the kindest way to destroy nations.

CHARITY IS POWERLESS

On any given day, anywhere around the world, thousands of middle-class citizens are harassed by wide-eyed puppets in polo shirts wearing lanyards, holding clipboards, trying to guilt us into a donation for a cause they've deemed worthy. We are bombarded on the streets, at the entrances of grocery stores and coffee shops, not to mention the visually emotional appeals via social media, TV, billboards, and direct mail. We are made to believe this is what we ought to be doing, that making a financial commitment is the right thing do, when all evidence alludes to the contrary.

Despite over $2 trillion in foreign aid dispensed from Western nations during the post–World War II era, approximately 40 percent of the world's population still live on less than two dollars per day. The story in North American communities is similar, with one initiative after another failing to meet its intended objectives. Indeed, over half a century after President Lyndon Johnson launched the War on Poverty, the poverty rate in America stubbornly hovers around 12 percent, decade after decade, year after year[13].

During the four decades leading up to the devastating earthquake of 2010, over $8 billion in foreign aid flowed into Haiti. The earthquake crisis surged additional aid commitments by another $13.5 billion from thirty-nine countries. Yet, four years later, the country had nothing to show for it — the national poverty rate remaining close to 59%[14]. Between 1970 and 1998, when aid flows to Africa were at their peak, the poverty rate in Africa *rose* from 11 percent to a staggering 66 percent[15].

Despite our most charitable efforts, the world's poor are not emerging from poverty. The poverty gap in the United States is increasing. Across the globe, in those lands where our aid is most concentrated, the poor are getting poorer[16]. Donations don't move the needle. Why?

Perhaps the manifestations of poverty are a reflection of something deeper; that the physical is merely a byproduct of the psychological. After all, if poverty was an issue of resource, charity would have solved it decades ago. Instead, it failed miserably. Trillions of dollars didn't make a dent.

Charity is only effective at addressing the *symptoms* of poverty: food, water, clothing, etc. Charity has no influence over the deep psychological matters that cause such calamities in the first place. As a result, it is powerless to stop it.

Surprisingly, while poor people do mention having a lack of possessions, they tend to describe their condition in far greater psychological and social terms. Poor people typically speak of shame, inferiority, powerlessness, humiliation, fear, hopelessness, depression, social isolation and voicelessness, more so than a lack of material things like food, money, clean water, medicine, housing, etc[17]. The mental strain of such emotions is difficult to bear, and bound to influence the psyche in adverse manners. Indeed, poverty of the mind seems to take a greater toll than its physical counterpart, and in ways we don't expect.

A small Texas church group on a mission trip to Nicaragua had the opportunity to witness the on-ground conditions at La Chureca, a waste-disposal site. What they saw touched them deeply: ill-clad urchins combing through mountains of garbage, hoping to find enough sellable rubbish to trade for a morsel of food; women dragging heavy bags of trash to makeshift sorting areas; men scooping up armfuls of heaping refuse. The filth, the stench, the disease: these images were burned indelibly into the conscience of the compassionate visitors. Something simply had to be done, the Texans concluded. It had to be something significant, more than typical service project activities or suitcases full of clothes; something that would permanently change the lives, the future, of these desperately poor people.

Over the following months, they organized a task force, assembled a plan, raised money, bought rural land, and designed a new, wholesome community for the people of La Chureca, far from the stench of the refuse pit. Each little home would have enough land to grow food to feed a family. In this healthy rural environment, parents could pursue time-honored farming traditions while their children breathed clean air, bathed in and drank ample pure water, and developed their minds at a nearby school.

Hundreds of volunteers mobilized around the project, both back home and in Nicaragua. Architects designed, engineers researched, marketers promoted, planners organized. Energy was high and money flowed. Soon dozens of homes were springing out of the ground; sturdy little homes that would protect against the monsoon winds and rains.

The mood at the dedication ceremony was euphoric. Scores of volunteers flew in for the event. Emotional prayers of thanksgiving were lifted heavenward. Praise music reverberated from loudspeakers. The smiling "New La Chureca" families in their freshly donated clothes posed proudly in front of their homes. It was almost like a new era had begun for them. Almost.

Two years later, all the families were living back at the dump[18].

A mission group returning from Haiti recounted a similar experience. Moved by compassion on seeing mothers carrying infants wrapped in dirty rags and newspapers, they purchased blankets and distributed them to the mothers. Less than 24 hours later, the blankets appeared in the shops along the street, having been sold by the mothers to local merchants[19].

People are more comfortable with the familiar than they are with the favorable. It's why homeless folks still sleep on the floor despite being given a bed at a shelter. It's why so many ex-convicts go back to prison shortly after release. It's why the people of La Chureca returned to the dump in the face of brand-new homes. Remarkably, we seem to be fine with this vain, cyclical arrangement. We don't care to look deeper into the origins of the issues. We merely want to adjust the scenery without doing the grunt work of uncovering how it came to be in the first place. As a society, we are almost exclusively fixated on the outward appearance of poverty, not what lies underneath. It's why charity continues to exist.

This is the vicious cycle of charity. The cycle that, in fact, perpetuates underdevelopment and guarantees economic failure in the poorest aid-dependent countries[20]. By focusing on the symptoms rather than the source, it ensures poverty will remain with us for generations. By failing to address the root cause, the threat of civil decay rises with quiet contingency.

TL;DR

As paradoxical as it may sound, charity does far more damage than we could expect or imagine. Instead of sustained development, deep relationships and mutual empowerment, all that is offered is momentary assistance, casual engagement and communal degradation. It delivers fulfillment and gratification to the benefactor, at the expense of the recipient.

Charity is perverse.

7

COMMON SENSE IS NONEXISTENT

Thinking is the hardest work many people have to do, and they don't like to do any more of it than they can help.

— Charles Zueblin

WHERE DO OUR THOUGHTS COME FROM?

For the most part, the world is what it is because human beings tend to share the same attitudes and perspectives on many issues and affairs. Despite our differences, whereabouts, upbringings and experiences, people often hold common views and judgements on most areas of life; even across multiple cultures and civilizations. It could be what most of us frequently refer to as "common sense" — despite the classical definition of the term — but while we hold common thoughts, they typically don't make sense.

. . .

The majority of folks don't know how to think; not critically at least. Any random individual would be hard-pressed to defend their worldview with any coherence, and don't ground most (if any) of their decisions in logic, rationale or reason.

Critical thinking is the most underrated skill in the world. It may be difficult to imagine, but almost every problem, misfortune and tragedy in the world, past and present, can be traced back to points of irrational thought or logical fallacy.

Faulty thinking stems from many diverse sources — religious dogma, ancestral tradition, political propaganda, commercial misinformation, emotional uncertainty, cultural superstition, widespread miseducation — there are too many active culprits to identify a leading one. Nevertheless, they are real, and yes, you and I are prone to such thinking in certain areas of our lives, whether we are aware of it or not.

OUR THINKING IS BROKEN

I've been wrong before. So have you. Fortunately, it's not a phenomenon limited to the two of us. Anyone who's ever lived has been wrong, multiple times, on many fronts, across the entire span of their existence. 100% of humans are capable and susceptible to failure, error and wrongdoing. In fact, if we are alive, it is inevitable. It goes without saying that some missteps are of greater consequence than others; our history on record makes that clear.

"Sidereus Nuncius" was a booklet published on March 13, 1610 by astronomer and physicist Galileo Galilei. The short publication (translated 'Starry Messenger') revealed some rather interesting discoveries he'd recently made with his telescope, among them, that the Earth was *not* the center of the universe[1]. Geocentrism was wrong. Earth revolved around the sun. This was quite a momentous and remarkable revelation at the time; there was just one problem: The observation was a seeming contradiction to the biblical understanding of the motion of the Earth.

As a result, in 1633, Galileo was summoned by the Roman Catholic Inquisition. Under threat of torture, Galileo was forced to recant his theory that the Earth moves around the Sun. He was forced to dismiss his own scientific findings as "abjured, cursed and detested", a renunciation that caused him great personal anguish, but which saved him from being burned at the stake[2]. It was only 359 years later, in late 1992, when the Catholic Church finally conceded. At a ceremony in Rome, before the Pontifical Academy of Sciences, Pope John Paul II officially declared that Galileo, the father of modern science, was right. It was the Inquisition who was wrong[3].

Up until the 19th century, bloodletting was a common and accepted remedy for curing a wide variety of ailments. Draining blood that was "bad" or "stagnant" was thought to be an effective method of purging disease. Bloodletting was used to treat everything from acne, to diabetes, to pneumonia, to cancer[4]. In 1799, George Washington, suffering from a throat infection, requested that his physician drain five pints of blood. He died a few hours later[5]. This form of treatment had gone unchallenged for over 2500 years, and it was only in the mid 1850s when bloodletting finally began to substantially decline, mainly for the efforts of one pathologist, John Hughes Bennett. As therapeutics moved towards a more science-based approach, not surprisingly, few physicians were anxious to announce to the public or admit to themselves that they and their predecessors had, for years, followed a theory that dictated an incorrect, worthless, and possibly injurious practice[6].

I don't intend to list every public dark age-esque error of the past, nor describe how they have held humanity back for centuries and stagnated our ability to progress as a civilization. Such a file would be too great and wide-ranging. However, it should no longer be difficult to imagine how any singular glitch in our rationale can cause widespread damage to the growth and development of society as a whole; especially if we don't detect and dismiss them as they surface.

Well, you might argue, "We're much smarter than our predecessors", or, "We don't have to worry about mass ignorance anymore". Alas, the data says otherwise. We may have slightly improved as a species, but there are still entire nations at war over false creeds and doctrines. People are still put to death for faux crimes such as blasphemy, apostasy, and homosexuality. Children are still indoctrinated to where their education is to recite from an ancient book of religious fiction. There are countries where women are denied almost every human liberty, except the liberty to breed[7]. In many ways, we don't look too different from the humans of old, and our cerebral transgressions are wildly oblivious to us.

How do we verifiably know if we are right, or wrong? Our thought processes are instinctively flawed, after all. And since we are naturally ignorant about most subjects and disciplines, we are prone to fall victim to various prejudices, biases and other cognitive traps when arriving at particular conclusions. Some of the most common fallacies to be aware of would include:

AD HOMINEM: To attack a person presenting an argument, rather than the substance of the argument itself e.g. *X person never graduated college, therefore his theory about Y must be wrong.*

The truth of an argument is independent of the character of the individual who asserts it, and should be assessed on its own merits.

AD POPULUM: To accept a proposition as true because many/most people believe it to be e.g. *X number of people believe in Y, therefore it must be true.*

There is no safety in numbers; the facts are the only thing that matter. To quote W. Somerset Maugham, "If 50 million people say something foolish, it's still foolish".

AD VERECUNDIAM: To use the opinion of a subject authority to support an argument e.g. *X professionals recommend product Y, therefore it must be the best.*

An expert opinion is no substitute for evidence. Authorities must prove their contentions like everybody else.

The list of logical errors we are aware of, and the propensity to commit any which one of them, at any time, is staggering. Expectedly, some are innocuous, while others are dangerous on a gradual level. One transgression in particular — that poses a threat to society en masse — is where we accept a practice based on its correlation to past or present traditions: AD ANTIQUITATEM.

. . .

If you've ever justified, defended or partaken in a questionable custom or ritual because "we've always done it this way", you're as guilty as the rest of us. For some strange reason, we hold tradition in such high regard that we never dare question it, even though we absolutely should. In reality, no singular tradition should be immune from scrutiny, whether it originated 5000 years ago, or just over the past few generations. If it doesn't serve us, it needs to go.

Unbeknownst to us, sound reasoning and judgement tend to fly out the window the moment we contemplate the practices of the past, whether it be rooted in religious, cultural, familial or societal norms. Considering any custom as sacred simply because it was so in the past is no reason to continue doing so. If anything, it is all the more reason we should frequently reevaluate them. Not only are most of them bankrupt of any tangible benefit, the time and energy they consume deem them worthy of disposal. This would also include the benign manifestations of tradition, like saying "bless you" after a sneeze, changing a last name post-marriage, clinking glasses with someone etc., which are more of an obligatory nuisance than anything else.

The dark, egregious and inhumane side of tradition arises when we observe ancient practices that cause irreparable damage, yet remain unquestioned and unchallenged. Objectively speaking, there doesn't seem to be any legitimate reason to accept, excuse or condone such needless formalities in the modern world. For example:

Shaking hands, which dates back to the 5th century B.C.[8] as a means to show you were not holding a weapon, poses a health risk[9] and is a breeding ground for germs and disease[10].

Every month, 14 infants die[11] from circumcision, which continues to claim the lives of new-born children all over the world. Any supposed argument for hygiene or cleanliness are contested (certainly not at risk of death), and there is evidence to show prolonged issues of psychological trauma[12] and premature ejaculation[13] being closely tied to circumcised men.

55% of marriages that occur around the world today are arranged[14], and 12 million forced marriages transpire every year[15]. Right now, at this very moment, young people around the globe are actively being stripped of their right to a full, free, and informed agreement to wed who they choose. They are dehumanized to the point of a mere bargaining chip, exchanged and leveraged for any sort of unscrupulous intention.

Tradition is a relic of a time gone by. In the modern world, they derail our progress, causing more affliction than advantage. To recognize and rescind such distraction, once and for all, is a critical duty for the human race — leaving the errors of the past where they belong — not carrying the remnants of our ignorance into the future with us.

A fitting allegory of tradition (and its relevance) would be the tale of Grandmother's Ham:

> A husband and wife were in their kitchen at home. The husband was sitting at the kitchen table, reading a newspaper, while his wife was preparing ham for dinner. The husband noticed his wife cutting off each end of the ham. He asked why she cut the ends off, proclaiming "That's a waste of good ham!", to which she replied "I don't know. That's the way my mother prepared the ham". The husband then asked, "Why did your mom cut the ends off?" — The wife didn't know.
>
> This seemed to bother her, so some time later, she called her mom to find out why she cut the ends of the ham off. Her mom answered, "I don't know. That's the way *my* mother prepared the ham".
>
> Undeterred, she made a late-night call to her grandmother. With some valor, she asked, "Grandma why do you cut the ends off the ham before cooking it?". Her grandmother replied, "We had a very small oven, and the

ham didn't fit in the oven, so I would cut the ends off".

Wasting food to ignorance, while symbolic, is near microscopic to what is lost on a global scale from our senseless rites and rituals. Without intervention, they may continue for ages. They simply cannot transfer from generation to generation without intentional review; they need to *earn* their way into the lives of autonomous human beings, and not come factory-installed through heredity.

Rationale is the way to sound thinking. But it's much more scarce than we realize. After all, if all human beings were rational, we wouldn't drink soda, smoke cigarettes or buy lottery tickets. We wouldn't believe in zodiac signs, homeopathy or feng shui. And we almost certainly wouldn't entertain superstitions like:

- Cell phone radiation causes cancer
- Going outside with wet hair causes colds
- Nazars protect us from the 'evil eye'
- Four-leaf clovers give us luck
- Coins in a fountain grant wishes
- The number 13 is unlucky
- Opening an umbrella indoors is wrong
- Breaking a mirror brings misfortune
- Bird droppings are a good sign

Yet, we're flawed. We believe in things we really shouldn't, and we never pause to reflect on our positions. We never stop to wonder if we're ever wrong. In fact, we almost always think we're right. As author Kathryn Schulz articulates, "*A whole lot of us go through life assuming that we are basically right, basically all the time, about basically everything: about our political and intellectual convictions, our religious and moral beliefs, our assessment of other people, our memories, our grasp of facts. As absurd as it sounds when we stop to think about it, our steady state seems to be one of unconsciously assuming that we are very close to omniscient*"[16]. It's not just a profound quote; the evidence backs it up:

65% of people believe they have above average intelligence[17].

73% of drivers believe they are better than average[18].

90% of professors believe that they are better than average[19].

94% of managers believe their listening skills are better than average[20].

The chances that a small business will survive for five years in the United States are about 35%. The individuals who start such businesses, however, estimate their chances at 60% — almost double the true value — and 33% believe their chance of failing is zero[21].

Do we suffer from delusions of grandeur? Or are we notoriously naive? Perhaps an outright concoction of the two. What we know for sure, is that we are in a continuous state of error. We are wrong more times than we are right. While we famously remember

Descartes penning the words, *Cogito ergo sum* (I think, therefore I am), we forget that twelve hundred years before that, Augustine wrote, *Fallor ergo sum* (I err, therefore I am)[22].

Error is our very nature. Any suggestion to the contrary is illusory.

OUR THINKING IS FIXED

So, what does it feel like to be wrong?

We tend to answer this question with words like painful, embarrassing, awkward or unpleasant. In actual fact, these words only describe what it feels like the moment *we realize* we are wrong. Until that moment, the feeling of being wrong is indistinguishable from the feeling of being right. We are all wrong about many things at every moment, but until we know it, we are confident that we are not[23]. Once we realize we are wrong, the logical next step is to admit it, thank those who may have helped us recognize it, and move on. But we do nothing of the sort, because we really aren't the sensible species we would like to think we are.

Professor, psychologist & author Jonathan Haidt has observed that when facts conflict with our values, *"almost everyone finds a way to stick with their own values and reject the evidence"*[24]. Further, when confronted by hard evidence that they're off the mark, some will simply double-down on their original assertion, rather than accept their error. This is the "backfire effect", where people increase their efforts to keep their own internal narrative consistent, despite clear indications they are wrong[25].

Why don't we respond to facts with logic? Why do we find it so difficult to accept new ideas and theories in light of new knowledge? There may be more reasons than we imagine:

INTELLECTUAL

When social psychologists David Dunning and Justin Kruger published a study on skill and awareness[26], they effectively discovered that the less intelligent we are in a particular domain, the more we seem to overestimate our actual intelligence in that domain. This hypothesis is known as the Dunning-Kruger Effect — basically, the dumber we are, the more confident we are that we're smart.

In the words of the philosopher Bertrand Russell, *"The fundamental cause of the trouble is that in the modern world, the stupid are cocksure, while the intelligent are full of doubt"*[27]. Those who are certain of their positions and unwilling to accept opposing evidence are perhaps the most uninformed and unaware of their own ignorance.

SOCIAL

In many scenarios, it would be beneficial to believe a falsity in order to remain within our tribes (family, friends, faith, culture, politics, neighborhood, school, sports). Sometimes, we just believe things because they keep us close to the people we care about. Kevin Simler sums it up well: *"If a brain anticipates that it will be rewarded for adopting a particular belief, it's perfectly happy to do so, and doesn't much care where the reward comes from — whether it's pragmatic (better outcomes resulting from better decisions), social (better treatment from one's peers), or some mix of the two*"[28].

Turning away from falsehood could very well mean being ostracized and denounced by the groups we seek to belong to. Practically speaking, very few would risk their comfort and security, in exchange for the unbiased and objective truth.

IDENTITY

Some of us, unfortunately, have our beliefs directly tied to our identity. Attacks on the ideology we subscribe to are misinterpreted as an attack on us personally. Neuroscientists find that when our core beliefs are challenged, it triggers the amygdala, the primitive "lizard brain" that breezes right past cool rationality and activates a hot fight-or-flight response[29].

When we define ourselves by our ideas, the thought of changing them is akin to losing a vital aspect of our character, personality or purpose. Thus, we reject truths when they pose a threat to our firmly held convictions. Even as articles of evidence continue to gather in the opposing direction, we cannot bring ourselves to evolve and embrace the zeitgeist. If only we could understand that it is our values that define us — not what we currently believe — we could remain objective about reality and perceive ideas as wholly independent from us; we can adopt or abandon them at any time, wherever the evidence leads us.

. . .

SUNK COST

Have you ever purchased tickets to a film screening, only to discover early into the movie that it has a confusing plot, insufferable dialogue and subpar acting? The logical move would be to simply walk out of the theater and make better use of your time. Most of us, though, would watch the movie to the end in order to justify the $20 we spent on the ticket. This concept is known as the "sunk cost effect", which describes how human beings irrationally continue in a task, endeavor or opinion because they have invested some deal of time or energy into it, despite all indications it should be dropped and discarded.

We make poor decisions, pursue worthless rewards and put ourselves at risk when we succumb to the sunk cost fallacy. Call it pride, ego or stubbornness, they all arise from the same state of mind: *"I've invested too much in this thing to walk away now"*. It applies to anyone, but especially to those who've made their ideas public e.g. religious leaders who deliver sermons, authors who write books, professors who publish articles, as well as adherents who've spent years of their lives entrenched in specific ideologies; the sunk cost sensation intensifies in direct correlation to the resources invested in it. And it takes a great deal of courage and self-awareness to remove ourselves from it.

With so many reasons and factors at play, is it ever a wonder why so many of us hold a fixed perspective, rarely able to break free from what we hold to be true?

When Socrates taught his students, he didn't try to stuff them full of knowledge. Instead, he sought to fill them with aporia: a sense of doubt, perplexity, and awe in the face of the complexity and contradictions of the world[30]. He thought it was his job to sting, to disturb, to question, and thereby to provoke his fellow Athenians to think through their current beliefs and change the ones they could not defend[31]. While there are many who hold a false worldview, we may find they hold such positions loosely, and are willing to reconsider their positions if only questioned. Like a teetering tower of Jenga, some gentle poking is all that is needed to break it down. As one apologist would argue: People don't know what they mean much of the time. Often, they're merely repeating slogans. When you ask them to flesh out their concern, opinion, or point of view with more precision, they're struck mute. They are forced to think, maybe for the first time, about exactly what they do mean[32].

Nevertheless, there is no shame in the admission of holding false beliefs for any period of time. What is of greater importance, is to see how we respond to new information that contradicts our beliefs. Rigid denial in the face of compelling evidence is the greatest thought crime we can commit. Conversely, it is utterly commendable to observe a public concession — a change of mind — to the point where others are willing to overlook wrongdoings associated with previous beliefs, when a better one is embraced. In fact, in all cases, it is wholeheartedly celebrated.

Take, for example, the story of a respected elder statesman of the Zoology Department at Oxford. As the story goes, for years he had passionately believed and taught that the Golgi Apparatus (a microscopic feature of the interior of cells) was not real: an artefact or illusion. Every week, it was the custom for the whole department to listen to a research talk by a visiting lecturer. One day, the visitor was an American cell biologist who presented completely convincing evidence that the Golgi Apparatus was real. At the end of the lecture, the old man strode to the front of the hall, shook the American by the hand and said — with passion — "*My dear fellow, I wish to thank you. I have been wrong these 15 years*". The students clapped their hands red[33].

Another case is from the early 1990s, when British physicist Andrew Lyne published a major discovery in the world's most prestigious science journal. He presented the first evidence that a planet could orbit a neutron star — a star that had exploded into a supernova. Several months later, while preparing to give a presentation at an astronomy conference, he noticed that he hadn't adjusted for the fact that the Earth moves in an elliptical orbit, not a circular one. He was embarrassingly, horribly wrong. The planet he had discovered didn't exist. In front of hundreds of colleagues, Andrew walked onto the ballroom stage and admitted his mistake. When he finished his confession, the room exploded in a standing ovation[34].

This occurrence is not limited to British scientists. One man by the name of Daryl Davis was able to (directly and indirectly) convince 200+ members of the Klu Klux Klan to renounce their bigoted beliefs and quit the organization altogether[35]. Although much of the credit goes to Daryl for his bravery as a black man to persist and engage in such hostile environments, it is equally admirable for a Klan member of any rank to contemplate their worldview, then make the monumental decision to abandon their long-affixed ideology, not to mention the social group they were welcomed and celebrated in for such a long period of time.

Megan Phelps-Roper, a lifelong member of the Westboro Baptist Church (an established hate group), was ultimately persuaded by random strangers on Twitter to conclusively reject the contradictory and inconsistent beliefs she was programmed to follow from a young age. After much correspondence — being unable to reconcile her doubts with her doctrine — Megan left the church, despite it meaning she would be shunned from her family forever. From once engaging in inflammatory homophobic and anti-American pickets, she now works with law enforcement agencies to combat extremist groups.

. . .

If the brainwashed and the indoctrinated have the capacity to think critically, weigh evidence against each other, and arrive at logical conclusions based on reason and rationale, so can plebs and commoners like you & I. There is no excuse.

By default, our minds are mostly fixed, but they shouldn't stay that way; especially if we want to grow as individuals and as a species. As playwright George Bernard Shaw noted, progress is impossible without change. And those who cannot change their minds, cannot change anything.

OUR THINKING IS FIXABLE

Are we all able to change our mind? Is such a feat even feasible for the average man?

Yes, and yes! Thanks to something known as "neuroplasticity". In basic terms, neuroplasticity is the brain's natural ability to adapt, reorganize and create new neural connections & pathways. It's how we are able to craft new skills, store memories, learn languages, control emotions and even recover from psychological trauma. The cerebrum is much more malleable than we realize, readjusting ever-so-slightly with every strand of new information that enters the psyche. Neuroplasticity, in short, is what allows us to evolve as humans. Fortunately, it is available to all brain-wielding beings.

Another change catalyst triggers through the natural process of biological development; specifically, in regard to a part of the brain known as the prefrontal cortex. Considered the "executive center" of our being, it deals with reason, analysis, innovation, attention and inhibition (among other things). While arguably the most important component of gray matter, the prefrontal cortex does not develop entirely until we reach 25 years of age[36]. Prior to that, most of us aren't thinking with sense as much as we are feeling with emotion[37]. Our ability to form cohesive arguments is limited, and there's little we can do to circumvent or accelerate the process. Only when the prefrontal cortex is fully formed, can we think and reason productively.

Awareness of our cognitive potential is useful. However, it still does not lead us to better thoughts on their own. Fortunately, there are cognitive tools we can utilize to bolster our mental capacity and reasoning ability. The most common techniques would include the adoption of inductive and deductive methodologies:

DEDUCTIVE REASONING

Deductive reasoning is the process of reasoning from one or more statements (known as premises) to reach a logical conclusion. If all premises are true, the terms are clear, and the rules of deductive logic are followed, then the conclusion reached is necessarily true.

The following syllogism is a well-known and sound example of deductive reasoning:

> *All men are mortal*
> *Socrates is a man*
> *Therefore, Socrates is mortal*

The conclusion is true by necessity, since both premises are true. If the conclusion were to be false, it is because one of the premises was false, for example:

> *Only police officers eat donuts*
> *George eats donuts*
> *Therefore, George is a police officer*

Since the first premise is false, the conclusion is invalid. Such an argument is often labelled a "non sequitur", to mean 'it does not follow'. Logically speaking, each premise has to follow from the previous one. When there is a disconnect between any two premises, the entire conclusion falls apart.

INDUCTIVE REASONING

Inductive reasoning, on the other hand, is the use of experience and observation to arrive at a general truth. The conclusions of inductive reasoning are considered probable — but not assurance — of the truth of the conclusion. For instance:

> *When I eat spicy food, I hiccup*
> *When I eat spicy food, I sweat*
> *Therefore, I'm allergic to spice*

Inductive reasoning can lead to conclusions that are clearly wrong, too. This often happens when we mistake correlation with causation, or when we apply the particular to the general. Sometimes, the conclusion could be correct even if the premises are wrong.

In simpler terms: Deductive reasoning works from the more general to the more specific; Inductive reasoning moves from specific observations to broader generalizations.

. . .

Both forms of reasoning are helpful and pragmatic, with most of us already using them to some degree on a regular basis whether we are conscious of it or not. Evoking syllogisms and premises, though, is complex and redundant to those of us amidst the hubbub of everyday life. Very few would take the time to sit down and rationalize their positions with logic, let alone deconstruct opposing ones when they present themselves. In this case, to navigate such matters neatly and readily — to reason effectively — we can simply pose the following question for any assertion: *How did I arrive at this conclusion?*

When phrased in this manner, it spurs us to think critically. It moves us closer to evidence and logic, and further away from bias and blind faith. Similar to the scales of justice, this simple question brings us back to impartiality — a neutral state — where we can weigh the arguments on their own merit in order to make a verdict. In doing so, we become less susceptible of falling victim to manipulation, conditioning, lies, indoctrination, deception, or any other form of false persuasion. A well-stated question won't solve every argument, nor produce certainty of truth, but it leads us much of the way there. Anything beyond that is a mere plus.

Certainty is an unrealistic ideal. In actual fact, we cannot know anything about reality with total assurance; all we have are probabilities. Nothing is absolute. Certainty, beyond the fact that you were born and you will one day die, does not exist[38]. As French philosopher Charles Renouvier once noted: *"There is no certainty; there are only people who are certain"*[39]. Despite our natural human desire for certainty, we are better off with basic probability. The presence of certainty signals the absence of discovery. When we are certain of select ideas and theories, we become intolerant of all others, which can lead to drastic outcomes. We've observed it many times throughout history: the vilest of deeds were committed by those with the utmost certainty[40]. Doubt, it seems, can be more of a friend than we appreciate.

What may come as disheartening news, is that we can utilize all our empirical wisdom and sensible logic, reasoning skills and cognitive abilities, and *still* come up short on where the truth lies. Some issues are far too intricate to explore, or rooted far too back in history to investigate. It could partly explain why so many people still believe in religion, conspiracy theories, mythical creatures & pseudoscience.

There is an intrinsic desire amongst humans to fill gaps of knowledge with something familiar or favorable, even if that thing is completely bogus. We may be inclined to classify these people as ignorant, feeble-minded hoi polloi. However, there *are* subsets of such individuals who have applied logic and reason to arrive at their conclusions. For example, theists who ground their faith in the 5 arguments for God[41] are worlds apart from archetypal religious folk, who's faith predominantly derives from their parent's chronic influence. The 6% of the population who believe unicorns are real creatures[42] are not like the people who hypothesized the same conclusion many years earlier. As the story goes:

> The ancient nomadic people of Europe discovered strange objects washed up along their shores. These objects were long, pointed, conical and had the weight and texture of bone. The nomads inferred that they must have been the horn of some kind of animal. The only animals they knew of with horns were land animals like the antelope and the elk. But these horns looked like they could not belong to either. The ancient nomads would have proposed the best possible explanation for what animal the horns might have belonged to, by observing their own surroundings and reasoning things out. So, they concluded the best explanation was that the horns must have belonged to a large and powerful species of horse that roamed some far away land.
>
> A horse was a land creature, and it was large enough and strong enough to bare the weight of the big horn. Since the horns were found washed up on shore, the nomads would have thought that these large horses died at sea, their bodies were devoured by sea beasts and that the horns floated to their coastal waters. And that is how the myth of the unicorn came about.

Many years later, it was discovered that the horns were not horns, but tusks; belonging to a small whale we know today as the 'narwhal'. As more evidence was brought forth against the unicorn hypothesis, the more the unicorn myth faded into obscurity.

The horns did belong to an animal, also a mammal, which died at sea, just as they had thought. It just so happens that the animal was not precisely the kind of animal they had imagined[43].

Despite the chances of being wrong, misguided and mistaken: by using simple logic and sound reasoning, we can be *less* wrong on most issues, as observed with the legend of the unicorn. When we question the premises of our conclusions, we can pinpoint where we slip up easier. When we ground our conclusions in logic, we can adjust our positions when new evidence arises.

Critical thought offers us cognitive freedom and flexibility; a way to amend our broken pathways and mental patterns. It is the roadmap to reality. If it is accurate to propose that devotion to the truth is the hallmark of morality[44], then critical thinking is the voice that guides us all along the path of righteousness.

TL;DR

Our cumulative ignorance on most subject matters, along with our propensity to deny error and fallacy in the face of sufficient evidence, make for a troubling concern in the effort to recondition society en masse. In the pursuit of creating a civilization where ignorance is a deliberate choice, most will continue to feel emotionally rather than think critically. Until logic and reason are adopted on a broad scale, the views we share will be questionable at best.

Common sense is nonexistent.

THIS IS YOUR LAST CHANCE

The mass of men lead lives of quiet desperation.

— Henry David Thorneu

How do you plan to live your life?

The information in this long-form essay is only as useful as the actions that follow it. This isn't just another amusing read on the metaphorical hamster wheel of education, self-improvement or entertainment; this is the literary catalyst for growth. This is the moment to make a choice.

Sadly, many will revert to their traditional way of life once they are done here. Most will not walk the road less traveled, afraid of the cuts and scars they will suffer from the pricks and thorns that await them off the beaten path. Plenty will cower to expectations set on them by friends, relatives, associates, and society at large. Not wanting to be judged for taking the less mainstream path and coming up empty[1], they will take the safe option every time, settling for a life of mediocrity and unfulfilled potential. The system still has them, and unfortunately, it will never let them go.

Let's be super crystal clear: Your life is yours, and yours alone. You don't owe anything to anyone, and are under no obligation to choose a certain lifestyle to appease any teacher, leader or parent. The concept of sonder[2] (the realization that every single person is living a life as vivid and complex as your own; populated with their own ambitions, friends, routines, worries and inherited craziness), articulates just how ridiculous our concerns about external opinions really are. People are innately too engrossed in matters of their own lives to ever make a clear judgment on yours. Any assessment they do provide is inadequate, lacking perspective and empathy. In other words, nobody has a credible say in the life you decide for yourself. Nobody.

But, you might ask, *What about respecting your elders?* The simple answer is no. Respect for anyone — of any age — is secondary to the respect you must exhibit toward yourself in remaining true to your values and desires.

. . .

Well, you may counter, *What about taking advice from those who are older and wiser?* Again, no. Nobody is wiser simply because they are older. Wisdom comes from learning, which comes from experience, which comes from trial and error. In other words, wisdom is in direct proportion to volume of action, struggle, failure, recovery and adaptation; not from total days on this earth. Heeding advice from someone solely due to their age is the pinnacle of stupidity.

The most revolutionary, pioneering, inspiring human beings who ever lived, all forged their own distinct path. They didn't seek permission, approval or acceptance from anyone. One such character, Steve Jobs, whose impact and influence on humanity endures on a level we may never completely fathom, had cautioned us:

When you grow up you, tend to get told that the world is the way it is and your life is just to live your life inside the world, try not to bash into the walls too much, try to have a nice family, save a little money.

That's a very limited life.

Life can be much broader, once you discover one simple fact, and that is that everything around you that you call life was made up by people that were no smarter than you. And you can change it, you can influence it, you can build your own things that other people can use.

Once you learn that, you'll never be the same again[3].

. . .

Of course, going your own way comes with its own set of doubts and adversity. Let's take Orny Adams for example:

Orny was an up-and-coming comedian from the suburban town of Lexington, Massachusetts. At the age of 29, after many years of hardship along with some mild success, he was frustrated and ready to give up, seeing everyone close around him succeed, while he remained relatively unknown as a comic. One night, at a comedy club where himself and the legendary Jerry Seinfeld were performing, Orny began to vent to Seinfeld about his predicament, which Jerry handled rather appropriately:

Orny: You get to a point where you're like, "How much longer can I take it?"

Jerry: What, is time running out? Are you out of time?

Orny: I'm getting older.

Jerry: Oh, please.

Orny: I'm getting older. It's odd. Listen, I'm 29. I feel like I've sacrificed so much of my life. The last 3 years have been a blur.

Jerry: Do you have something else you would rather have been doing? You got other appointments or other places you gotta be?

Orny: Not necessarily, but-

Jerry: No, not necessarily.

Orny: I see all my friends are making a lot of money on Wall Street.

Jerry: What?

Orny: They're moving up. And I'm worried-

Jerry: They're moving up?

Orny: They're moving up.

Jerry: Are you out of your mind?

Orny: No! I'm not. I just uh-

Jerry: This is a special thing. This has nothing to do with "making it" or-

Orny: But, did you ever stop and compare your life? I'm 29, my friends are all married. They're all having kids. They all have houses. They have some sense of normality-

Jerry: (*wincing in disgust*) Ugh!

Orny: What do you tell your parents? How do you deal with that?

Jerry: What do you tell your parents? This is-

Realizing general encouragement and reassurance may not be enough to get through to him, Seinfeld proceeded to tell Orny his favorite anecdote about show biz, hoping it would impart some wisdom and perspective to the young comic. The story went something like this:

Glenn Miller's orchestra was performing a gig somewhere, but they could not land where they were supposed to because it was a snowy, winter night. So, they had to land in a nearby field and walk the rest of the way to the gig. They are already dressed in their suits, ready to play, and they're carrying their instruments.

As they're walking through the wet and slushy snow, in the distance, they see a little house, with the lights on, and a ball of smoke coming out of the chimney.

They walk up to the house, and they look in the window to see this family. Inside is a man and his wife; she's beautiful. There's two kids, and they're all sitting around the table, smiling and laughing; they're eating, and there's a fire in the fireplace.

Meanwhile, these musicians are standing outside in their suits; they're wet, they're shivering, holding onto their instruments, while watching this incredible Norman Rockwell scene.

At that moment, one of the guys turns to the other and says, "How do people *live* like that?"

The moral of the story is this: life has no instruction manual, and with good reason. There is no set path; no 'normal' way to live. Comparing your life to others is foolish when you innately hold differing goals, dreams and desires to everyone else. It is ridiculous to contrast yourself against others, when you stop for a moment to consider just how unique your traits, experiences and circumstances really are. All such measurements are frivolous.

None of this is to imply the alternative way of life is any easier. On the contrary, life in general, within or without the system, will most surely be one of immense pain and suffering. It is inescapable, no matter how diligent or careful we are. Realistically, you can't get rid of pain — pain is the universal constant of the human condition. Trying to eliminate pain will only increase your sensitivity to suffering, rather than alleviating your suffering[4].

On a balance of probabilities, you were dealt a bad hand in at least one area of life or another. It is what it is. Almost no one was given a perfect start. There are very few people who were born:

- With optimal health
- In a loving, two-parent family
- With natural beauty
- Into a set inheritance, via a business or trust fund
- In a country of freedom, prosperity, diversity and opportunity

Unfortunately, most of us have to deal with:

- Nagging health conditions, diseases, ailments and disorders
- Childhood trauma or abuse
- Pains of rejection, insecurity, discrimination and loneliness
- Working stressful, undesirable jobs for extended periods of time
- The toil and sacrifice of migration, poverty and lack

There will be those who are lazy and still prosper, while the earnest and diligent perpetually struggle. The beloved will die young, while the despicable live long. Indeed, life fails to make sense a lot of the time. It's unfair and unjust. But it's also the reality. The big question is: how will we respond?

The world is cold, dark and depressing. And while weeping may relieve some emotional stress[5], it doesn't do anything to alter the facts. Lamentation doesn't bring on the change we desire; action does. Ironically, the same energy we use to cry and complain about our circumstance, can instead be used to devise a way out of it. We may have lost some time leading up to this point, but we have no excuse not to begin the process of transformation right this moment. As the Chinese proverb goes, the best time to plant a tree was 20 years ago; the second best time is today[6].

This is your life, and it's ending one second at a time. It's yours to live, to take in any direction you see fit, with whomever you choose to live it with. Losing but another moment of it to fear, comparison or indignation is a painful curse of the most needless order.

Let's face it: one day, you and everyone you love will die. And beyond a small group of people for an extremely brief period of time, little of what you say or do will ever matter[7]. At some point in time, you will disappear from this earth, and there's nothing you can do about it. That may be hard to accept, but the truth is not what you want it to be; it is what it is. And you must bend to its power, or live a lie[8]. I don't know what your future holds, but I do know it will be better off in the perpetual awareness of this reality. Remembering that this whole thing ends is the highest motivation. The transience of your existence is the best incentive you could ever need to live life the way you really want.

The most fundamental aspect of your humanity is your ability to make choices and stand by those choices, what Viktor Frankl called the last of human freedoms; to *"choose one's own way"*[9]. Choosing one's own way is what makes one human, and the more you own the power of your own decision-making, the more your life and outcomes will be within your control[10].

The mistakes we ultimately regret are not errors of commission, but errors of omission. If we could do things over, almost all of us would censor ourselves less and express our ideas more[11]. This is your opportunity to begin to do just that. This is your moment to decide.

Where we go from here is a choice I leave to you

NOTES

The System Has You

1. "Semmelweis reflex", Wikipedia, September 10, 2020, https://en.wikipedia.org/wiki/Semmelweis_reflex
2. Leah Ginnivan, "The Dirty History of Doctors' Hands", Ohio State University, November 25, 2016, https://u.osu.edu/korzen.1/2016/11/25/the-dirty-history-of-doctors-hands/
3. Garson O'Toole, "If I Had More Time, I Would Have Written a Shorter Letter", Quote Investigator, April 28, 2012, https://quoteinvestigator.com/2012/04/28/shorter-letter/

1. Diamonds Are Worthless

1. M. Garside, "Global diamond jewelry market value 2009-2019", Statista, November 11, 2020, https://www.statista.com/statistics/585267/diamond-jewelry-market-value-worldwide/
2. Jennifer Chu, "Sound waves reveal diamond cache deep in Earth's interior", MIT News, July 16, 2018, https://news.mit.edu/2018/sound-waves-reveal-diamond-cache-deep-earths-interior-0716
3. Edward Jay Epstein, "Have You Ever Tried to Sell a Diamond?", The Atlantic, February 1, 1982, https://www.theatlantic.com/magazine/archive/1982/02/have-you-ever-tried-to-sell-a-diamond/304575/
4. "Argyle Diamonds", Visit Kununurra, https://www.visitkununurra.com/learn/argyle-diamonds
5. F. Verschoyle, *Cecil Rhodes: His Political Life and Speeches, 1881-1900.* (HardPress, 2018), 805.
6. Kevin Crowley, "De Beers Hoovers Up Its Best Diamonds From the African Seabed", Bloomberg, July 11, 2017, https://www.bloomberg.com/news/photo-essays/2017-07-11/de-beers-hoovers-up-its-best-diamonds-from-the-african-seabed
7. David G. Findley, "3-D Diamond Printing Using a Pre-Ceramic Polymer with a Nanoparticle Filler", US Patent & Trademark Office, July 28, 2016, https://appft.uspto.gov/netacgi/nph-Parser?Sect1=PTO1&Sect2=HITOFF&d=PG01&p=1&u=%2Fnetahtml%2FPTO%2Fsrchnum.html&r=1&f=G&l=50&s1=%2220160214272%22.PGNR.&OS=DN/20160214272&RS=DN/20160214272

8. Henry Sanderson, "Diamond Foundry valued at $1.8bn after $200m fundraising", Financial Times, April 26, 2021, https://www.ft.com/content/34254394-a1dd-42a0-8d95-e4dd39254eac
9. J. Courtney Sullivan, *The Engagements* (New York, Alfred A. Knopf, 2013), 8.
10. J. Courtney Sullivan, "How Diamonds Became Forever", The New York Times, May 3, 2013, https://www.nytimes.com/2013/05/05/fashion/weddings/how-americans-learned-to-love-diamonds.html
11. Robert Vare, *The American Idea* (New York, Broadway Books, 2008), 407.
12. Jay Epstein, "THE DIAMOND MIND", Edward Jay Epstein, May 10, 2011, http://edwardjayepstein.com/diamond/chap13_print.htm
13. Rohin Dhar, "Diamonds Are Bullshit", Priceonomics, June 23, 2014, https://priceonomics.com/post/45768546804/diamonds-are-bullshit
14. Hector Macdonald, *Truth: How the Many Sides to Every Story Shape Our Reality* (New York, Little Brown Spark, 2018).
15. Laurence Cawley, "De Beers myth: Do people spend a month's salary on a diamond engagement ring?", BBC News, May 16, 2014, https://www.bbc.com/news/magazine-27371208
16. Mackenzie Dawson, "How America was conned into buying diamonds", New York Post, June 11, 2016, https://nypost.com/2016/06/11/two-spinsters-a-single-mom-and-hollywood-conned-america-into-buying-diamonds/
17. J. Courtney Sullivan, "Why 'A Diamond Is Forever' has lasted so long", The Washington Post, February 7, 2014, https://www.washingtonpost.com/opinions/why-a-diamond-is-forever-has-lasted-so-long/2014/02/07/f6adf3f4-8eae-11e3-84e1-27626c5ef5fb_story.html
18. Gad Saad, *The Evolutionary Bases of Consumption*, (Abingdon, Routledge, 2007), 67.
19. Meghan O'Rourke, "Diamonds Are a Girl's Worst Friend", Slate, June 11, 2007, https://slate.com/news-and-politics/2007/06/engagement-rings-good-or-bad.html
20. Zachary Crockett, *Everything is Bullshit*, (San Francisco, Priceonomics, 2014), 3.
21. Megan Elliott, "Why It May Be a Mistake to Spend Big Money on an Engagement Ring", CheatSheet, June 15, 2015, https://www.cheatsheet.com/life/why-it-may-be-a-mistake-to-spend-big-money-on-an-engagement-ring.html/
22. Harry Campbell, "Why a Diamond Engagement Ring is NOT a Good Investment", SmartAsset, May 21, 2018, https://smartasset.com/credit-cards/why-a-diamond-engagement-ring-is-not-a-good-investment

23. Peter A. Stanwick, *Understanding Business Ethics* (Thousand Oaks, SAGE Publications Inc, 2015) 360.
24. Mike W. Peng, *Global Strategy* (Boston, Cengage Learning, 2013) 446.
25. "Diamonds as an investment", Wikipedia, https://en.wikipedia.org/wiki/Diamonds_as_an_investment
26. Joe Terzeon, "This is why diamonds aren't rare or valuable", VT, November 23, 2017, https://vt.co/lifestyle/diamonds-arent-rare-valuable/
27. Low, Rand & Yao, Yiran & Faff, Robert. (2015). Diamonds vs. Precious Metals: What shines brightest in your investment portfolio?. International Review of Financial Analysis. 43. http://doi.org/10.1016/j.irfa.2015.11.002
28. Rob Bates, "Are Diamonds a Waste of Money?", JCK, August 15, 2012, https://www.jckonline.com/editorial-article/are-diamonds-a-waste-of-money/

2. Marriage Is Toxic

1. Musick, K., & Bumpass, L. (2012). Re-Examining the Case for Marriage: Union Formation and Changes in Well-Being. Journal of marriage and the family, 74(1), 1–18. https://doi.org/10.1111/j.1741-3737.2011.00873.x
2. Nanci Hellmich, "Gain a Spouse and You'll Likely Gain Some Pounds, Too," USA Today, October 23, 2007, http://usatoday30.usatoday.com/news/health/2007-10-22-marriage-weight_N.htm
3. Helen Smith, *Men on Strike* (New York, Encounter Books, 2013), 11.
4. Chateau Heartiste, "Marriage Does A Body Bad", October 26, 2007, https://heartiste.org/2007/10/26/marriage-does-a-body-bad/
5. "Modern Marriage", Pew Research Social & Demographic Trends, July 18, 2007, https://www.pewsocialtrends.org/2007/07/18/modern-marriage/
6. Mark Regnerus, *Cheap Sex* (New York, Oxford University Press, 2017), 72.
7. David K. Li, "Straying Dogs", New York Post, May 19, 2008 https://nypost.com/2008/05/19/straying-dogs/
8. Mark Oppenheimer, "Married, With Infidelities", New York Times, June 30, 2011, https://www.nytimes.com/2011/07/03/magazine/infidelity-will-keep-us-together.html
9. Philip Weiss, "The Affairs of Men", New York Magazine, May 16, 2008, https://nymag.com/relationships/sex/47055/
10. Eirc Spitznagel, "Marriage Secrets from Prostitutes", Medium, January 9, 2019, https://espitznagel.medium.com/marriage-

secrets-from-prostitutes-8f6fe7f263cb
11. Bob Berkowitz, *He's Just Not Up for It Anymore* (New York, Harper Perennial, 2008), 4.
12. Baumeister, R. F., & Vohs, K. D. (2004). Sexual Economics: Sex as Female Resource for Social Exchange in Heterosexual Interactions. Personality and Social Psychology Review, 8(4), 339–363. https://doi.org/10.1207/s15327957pspr0804_2
13. Christopher Ryan, *Sex at Dawn* (New York, Harper Collins, 2010), 2.
14. "Marriage & divorce", American Psychological Association, https://www.apa.org/topics/divorce/
15. Rosenfeld, Michael J., Thomas, Reuben J., and Falcon, Maja (2016). How Couples Meet and Stay Together (HCMST), Wave 1 2009, Wave 2 2010, Wave 3 2011, Wave 4 2013, Wave 5 2015, United States. Ann Arbor, MI: Inter-university Consortium for Political and Social Research. https://doi.org/10.3886/ICPSR30103.v8
16. Røsand, G. M., Slinning, K., Røysamb, E., & Tambs, K. (2014). Relationship dissatisfaction and other risk factors for future relationship dissolution: a population-based study of 18,523 couples. Social psychiatry and psychiatric epidemiology, 49(1), 109–119. https://doi.org/10.1007/s00127-013-0681-3
17. RICHARDS, M., HARDY, R., & WADSWORTH, M. (1997). The effects of divorce and separation on mental health in a national UK birth cohort. Psychological Medicine, 27(5), 1121-1128. https://doi.org/10.1017/S003329179700559X
18. Lorenz, F. O., Wickrama, K. A. S., Conger, R. D., & Elder, G. H. (2006). The Short-Term and Decade-Long Effects of Divorce on Women's Midlife Health. Journal of Health and Social Behavior, 47(2), 111–125. https://doi.org/10.1177/002214650604700202
19. Leopold T. (2018). Gender Differences in the Consequences of Divorce: A Study of Multiple Outcomes. Demography, 55(3), 769–797. https://doi.org/10.1007/s13524-018-0667-6
20. Edwards, A. C., Larsson Lönn, S., Sundquist, J., Kendler, K. S., & Sundquist, K. (2018). Associations Between Divorce and Onset of Drug Abuse in a Swedish National Sample. American journal of epidemiology, 187(5), 1010–1018. https://doi.org/10.1093/aje/kwx321
21. Kiecolt-Glaser J. K. (2018). Marriage, divorce, and the immune system. The American psychologist, 73(9), 1098–1108. https://doi.org/10.1037/amp0000388
22. Dupre, M. E., George, L. K., Liu, G., & Peterson, E. D. (2015). Association between divorce and risks for acute myocardial infarction. Circulation. Cardiovascular quality and outcomes, 8(3), 244–251. https://doi.org/10.1161/CIRCOUTCOMES.114.001291

23. Alyssa Brown, "Separation, Divorce Linked to Sharply Lower Well-Being", Gallup, April 20 2012, https://news.gallup.com/poll/154001/Separation-Divorce-Linked-Sharply-Lower-Wellbeing.aspx
24. Kposowa, Augustine J (2000). Marital status and suicide in the National Longitudinal Mortality Study. Journal of Epidemiology & Community Health; 54:254-261. http://dx.doi.org/10.1136/jech.54.4.254
25. Kyle J Bourassa, MA, John M Ruiz, PhD, David A Sbarra, PhD, Smoking and Physical Activity Explain the Increased Mortality Risk Following Marital Separation and Divorce: Evidence From the English Longitudinal Study of Ageing, Annals of Behavioral Medicine, Volume 53, Issue 3, March 2019, Pages 255–266, https://doi.org/10.1093/abm/kay038
26. Schramm, D. Individual and Social Costs of Divorce in Utah. *J Fam Econ Iss* **27**, 133–151 (2006). https://doi.org/10.1007/s10834-005-9005-4
27. Forthofer, M., Markman, H., Cox, M., Stanley, S., & Kessler, R. (1996). Associations between Marital Distress and Work Loss in a National Sample. Journal of Marriage and Family, 58(3), 597-605, https://doi.org/10.2307/353720
28. Harper, C.C. and McLanahan, S.S. (2004), Father Absence and Youth Incarceration. Journal of Research on Adolescence, 14: 369-397. https://doi.org/10.1111/j.1532-7795.2004.00079.x
29. McDermott, R., Fowler, J., & Christakis, N. (2013). Breaking Up is Hard to Do, Unless Everyone Else is Doing it Too: Social Network Effects on Divorce in a Longitudinal Sample. Social forces; a scientific medium of social study and interpretation, 92(2), 491–519. https://doi.org/10.1093/sf/sot096
30. Andrew J. Cherlin, *The Marriage-Go-Round: The State of Marriage and the Family in America Today*, (New York, Vintage, 2010), 25.
31. Edrie Pfeiffer, "What Are The Statistics On Divorce In America?", Hampton Roads Legal Services, https://www.hamptonroadslegal.com/faqs/facts-on-divorce-in-america.cfm
32. Romans 11:13 *New International Version* (NIV)
33. 1 Corinthians 7:8 *New International Version* (NIV)
34. Ben Bradlee Jr., *The Kid: The Immortal Life of Ted Williams*, (New York, Little, Brown and Company, 2013), 345.
35. The University of Michigan, *The Electrical Journal, Volume 2, Issue 3* (Ann Arbor, Electrical Journal Publishing Company, 1896), 546.
36. Tom Crouch, *The Bishop's Boys: A Life of Wilbur and Orville Wright*, (New York: W. W. Norton & Company, 2003), 118.
37. "'It's not because I never had time': Oprah Winfrey reveals why she never married", Hello! Magazine, November 15, 2013,

https://www.hellomagazine.com/film/2013111515661/oprah-winfrey-talks-marriage-lorraine-kelly/

3. Employees Are Losers

1. Barnett AG, Dobson AJ. Excess in cardiovascular events on Mondays: a meta-analysis and prospective study (*Journal of Epidemiology & Community Health*) 2005; 59:109-114. http://dx.doi.org/10.1136/jech.2003.019489
2. Jim Harter, "Historic Drop in Employee Engagement Follows Record Rise", Gallup, July 2, 2020, https://www.gallup.com/workplace/313313/historic-drop-employee-engagement-follows-record-rise.aspx
3. Paula Brunoro, "What is the Average Jail Time for Tax Evasion?", Milikowsky Tax Law, August 20, 2020, https://www.caltaxadviser.com/blog/2020/08/what-is-the-average-jail-time-for-tax-evasion/
4. Tom Wheelwright, *Tax-Free Wealth: How to Build Massive Wealth by Permanently Lowering Your Taxes* (Scottsdale, RDA Press LLC, 2012), 43.
5. Tom Wheelwright, "Why You Should Fire Your CPA Today", Rich Dad, December 16, 2019, https://www.richdad.com/fire-cpa-today
6. Tony Robbins, *Unshakeable*, (New York, Simon & Schuster, 2018) 25.
7. Les Brown, *Live Your Dreams*, (New York, William Morrow Paperbacks, 1994), 194.
8. Nassim Nicholas Taleb, *The Bed of Procrustes: Philosophical and Practical Aphorisms*, (New York, Random House LLC, 2010), 51.
9. T. Harv Ecker, *Secrets of the Millionaire Mind: Mastering the Inner Game of Wealth*, (New York, HarperCollins, 2009), 172.
10. Katie Arnold, "Drafting Dean: Interview Outtakes", Outside, December 8, 2006, https://www.outsideonline.com/1885421/drafting-dean-interview-outtakes
11. MJ Demarco, *The Millionaire Fastlane: Crack the Code to Wealth and Live Rich for a Lifetime*, (Fountain Hills, Viperion Publishing, 2011), 47.
12. Moon JR, Glymour MM, Subramanian SV, Avendaño M, Kawachi I. Transition to retirement and risk of cardiovascular disease: prospective analysis of the US health and retirement study. Social Science & Medicine. 2012;75(3):526-530. https://doi.org/10.1016/j.socscimed.2012.04.004
13. Behncke S. Does retirement trigger ill health? Health Economics. 2012;21(3):282-300. https://doi.org/10.1002/hec.1712
14. Lucy Dayman, "Ikigai: The Japanese Concept Of Finding Purpose In Life", Savvy Tokyo, January 15, 2020, https://savvy

tokyo.com/ikigai-japanese-concept-finding-purpose-life/
15. Digital Daijisen, "Ikigai", Kotobank, https://kotobank.jp/word/生き甲斐-431174
16. Wu C, Odden MC, Fisher GG, et al. Association of retirement age with mortality: a population-based longitudinal study among older adults in the USA. J. Epidemiol Community Health. 2016;70:917-923. http://dx.doi.org/10.1136/jech-2015-207097
17. Kachan D, Fleming LE, Christ S, Muennig P, Prado G, Tannenbaum SL, et al. Health Status of Older US Workers and Nonworkers, National Health Interview Survey, 1997–2011. Preventing Chronic Disease. 2015;12:150040. http://dx.doi.org/10.5888/pcd12.150040
18. Garrett B. Gunderson, *Killing Sacred Cows: Overcoming the Financial Myths That Are Destroying Your Prosperity*, (Austin, Greenleaf Book Group LLC, 2008), 122.

4. School Is Child Abuse

1. Melanie Hanson, "College Enrollment & Student Demographic Statistics", Education Data, June 25, 2021, https://educationdata.org/college-enrollment-statistics
2. Richard Vedder, *Going Broke By Degree: Why College Costs Too Much*, (Washington D.C., AEI Press, 2004), 44.
3. Jon Marcus, "Bureaucratic costs at some colleges are twice what's spent on instruction", The Hechinger Report, July 25, 2017, https://hechingerreport.org/bureaucratic-costs-colleges-twice-whats-spent-instruction/
4. Shannon Insler, "Do Millennials Have It Better or Worse Than Generations Past?", Student Loan Hero, May 30, 2018, https://studentloanhero.com/featured/millennials-have-better-worse-than-generations-past/
5. Paul Fain, "Mixed Views on Higher Ed", Inside Higher Ed, May 11, 2017, https://www.insidehighered.com/news/2017/05/11/americans-see-value-higher-education-survey-finds-are-unhappy-current-system
6. Katy Steinmetz, "Move Over, Millennials: How Generation Z Is Disrupting Work As We Know It", Time, December 20, 2017, https://time.com/5066641/generation-z-disruption/
7. Malcolm Gladwell, *Outliers: The Story of Success*, (New York, Little Brown and Company, 2008), 41.
8. Brad Plumer, "Only 27 percent of college grads have a job related to their major", The Washington Post, May 20, 2013, https://www.washingtonpost.com/news/wonk/wp/2013/05/20/only-27-percent-of-college-grads-have-a-job-related-to-their-major/

9. Madilyn Smith, "Understanding the 8 Types Of Learning Styles", Mindvalley, January 16, 2019, https://blog.mindvalley.com/types-of-learning-styles/
10. Matthew M. Chingos, "Class Size: What Research Says and What it Means for State Policy", Brookings, May 11, 2011, https://www.brookings.edu/research/class-size-what-research-says-and-what-it-means-for-state-policy/
11. Schools and Staffing Survey (SASS), "Table 7. Average class size in public primary schools, middle schools, high schools, and schools with combined grades, by classroom type and state: 2011–12", National Center for Education Statistics, https://nces.ed.gov/surveys/sass/tables/sass1112_2013314_t1s_007.asp
12. Reichsparteitag, 1935.
13. Aristotle, *The Philosophy of Aristotle*, (London, Penguin, 2011).
14. Connor Boyack, *Passion-Driven Education: How to Use Your Child's Interests to Ignite a Lifelong Love of Learning*, (Lehi, Libertas, 2016), 83.
15. Julia Moeller, Marc A. Brackett, Zorana Ivcevic, Arielle E. White, High school students' feelings: Discoveries from a large national survey and an experience sampling study, Learning and Instruction,Volume 66, 2020, 101301, ISSN 0959-4752, https://doi.org/10.1016/j.learninstruc.2019.101301
16. John Taylor Gatto, *Dumbing Us Down: The Hidden Curriculum of Compulsory Schooling*, (Gabriola Island, New Society Publishers, 1992), 20.
17. John Taylor Gatto, *Weapons of Mass Instruction: A Schoolteacher's Journey Through the Dark World of Compulsory Schooling*, (Gabriola Island, New Society Publishers, 2009), 141.
18. John Taylor Gatto, "I quit, I think", The Wall Street Journal, July 25, 1991, https://www.educationrevolution.org/blog/i-quit-i-think/
19. Erica Goldson, "Valedictorian Speaks Out Against Schooling in Graduation Speech", Permaculture News, August 1, 2013, https://www.permaculturenews.org/2013/08/01/valedictorian-speaks-out-against-schooling-in-graduation-speech/
20. Leone, C.M., Richards, H. Classwork and homework in early adolescence: The ecology of achievement. *J Youth Adolescence* 18, 531–548 (1989). https://doi.org/10.1007/BF02139072
21. Csikszentmihalyi, M., Hunter, J. Happiness in Everyday Life: The Uses of Experience Sampling. *Journal of Happiness Studies* 4, 185–199 (2003). https://doi.org/10.1023/A:1024409732742
22. National Center for Education Statistics, "Bullying", 2017, https://nces.ed.gov/fastfacts/display.asp?id=719

23. Romano, I., Butler, A., Patte, K.A. et al. High School Bullying and Mental Disorder: an Examination of the Association with Flourishing and Emotional Regulation. *Int Journal of Bullying Prevention* (2019). https://doi.org/10.1007/s42380-019-00035-5
24. Vaughn, M. G., Salas-Wright, C. P., Kremer, K. P., Maynard, B. R., Roberts, G., & Vaughn, S. (2015). Are homeschooled adolescents less likely to use alcohol, tobacco, and other drugs?. *Drug and alcohol dependence*, 155, 97–104. https://doi.org/10.1016/j.drugalcdep.2015.08.010
25. Sarah Harris, "Winning is banned at more than half of primary school sports days: Pupils compete in teams despite 82% of parents wanting a traditional event", Daily Mail, July 5, 2017, https://www.dailymail.co.uk/news/article-4669512/Winning-banned-half-school-sports-days.html
26. "Safe space", Wikipedia, July 15, 2016, https://en.wikipedia.org/wiki/Safe_space
27. "Disinvitation Database", FIRE, 2020, https://www.thefire.org/research/disinvitation-database/
28. Ethel Tovar, "Students and parents pressure teachers to change grades", Deseret News, February 7, 2000, https://www.deseret.com/2000/2/7/19489626/students-and-parents-pressure-teachers-to-change-grades
29. Greg Lukianoff, *The Coddling of the American Mind: How Good Intentions and Bad Ideas Are Setting Up a Generation for Failure*, (London, Penguin, 2018), 23.

5. Passion Is Overrated

1. Mike Rowe, "Saturday Mail Call", Facebook, April 19, 2014, https://www.facebook.com/TheRealMikeRowe/posts/773954069281405
2. Bill Burnett, Designing Your Life: How to Build a Well-Lived, Joyful Life, (New York, Knopf, 2016), 29.
3. Angela Duckworth, *Grit: The Power of Passion and Perseverance*, (New York, Scribner, 2016), 104.
4. Eric Barker, "Research Shows These Four Things Will Make You A Peak Performer", Barking Up The Wrong Tree, June 15, 2012, https://www.bakadesuyo.com/2012/06/what-type-of-practice-produces-peak-performan/
5. Roediger, H. L. III, Agarwal, P. K., McDaniel, M. A., & McDermott, K. B. (2011). Test-enhanced learning in the classroom: Long-term improvements from quizzing. Journal of Experimental Psychology: Applied, 17(4), 382–395. https://doi.org/10.1037/a0026252
6. Marie Forleo, *Everything is Figureoutable*, (London, Portfolio, 2019), 121.

7. David Epstein, *Range: Why Generalists Triumph in a Specialized World*, (New York, Riverhead Books, 2019), 66.
8. Ross Tucker, "Ross Tucker on Twitter", Twitter, November 7, 2017, https://twitter.com/Scienceofsport/status/927959162268585984
9. Brené Brown, *Braving the Wilderness: The Quest for True Belonging and the Courage to Stand Alone* (New York, Random House, 2019), 40.
10. Barry Schwartz, *The Paradox of Choice: Why More Is Less*, (New York, HarperCollins, 2009), 141.
11. Scott Adams, *How to Fail at Almost Everything and Still Win Big: Kind of the Story of My Life* (New York, Penguin, 2014), 21.
12. Jordan Raynor, *Master of One: Find and Focus on the Work You Were Created to Do*, (Colorado Springs, WaterBrook, 2020), 64.
13. Benjamin P. Hardy, *Personality Isn't Permanent: Break Free from Self-Limiting Beliefs and Rewrite Your Story*, (London, Portfolio, 2020), 52.
14. Chen, P., Ellsworth, P. C., & Schwarz, N. (2015). Finding a Fit or Developing It: Implicit Theories About Achieving Passion for Work. Personality and Social Psychology Bulletin, 41(10), 1411–1424. https://doi.org/10.1177/0146167215596988
15. Brad Stulberg, *The Passion Paradox: A Guide to Going All In, Finding Success, and Discovering the Benefits of an Unbalanced Life*, (New York, Rodale Books, 2019), 37.
16. Anders Ericsson, *Peak: Secrets from the New Science of Expertise*, (New York, First Mariner Books, 2017), 180.
17. "Judit Polgar – I just can't live without chess", Chessdom, November 26, 2009, http://interviews.chessdom.com/judit-polgar-khanty-mansiysk
18. Kevin Habits, "More brilliance from Scott Adams: 'You want the grinder, not the guy who loves his job'", Kevin Habits, February 22, 2017, https://kevinhabits.com/more-brilliance-from-scott-adams-you-want-the-grinder-not-the-guy-who-loves-his-job/
19. Geoff Colvin, *Talent is Overrated: What Really Separates World-Class Performers from Everybody Else*, (New York, Portfolio, 2010), 23.
20. T. W. Smith, *Solid Ground: A Foundation for Winning in Work and in Life*, (Scottsdale, T. W. Lewis Company, 2020), 120.
21. Jason Hreha, "This Cognitive Trap Is Your Biggest Barrier to Success", Inc, November 30, 2016, https://www.inc.com/jason-hreha/this-cognitive-trap-is-your-biggest-barrier-to-success.html
22. Barry Brownstein, "Effort Matters: The Pioneering Work of Anders Ericsson", American Institute for Economic Research, July 29, 2020, https://www.aier.org/article/effort-matters-the-pioneering-work-of-anders-ericsson/

23. Chad Aldeman, "What the Education Sector Can Learn from Peak: Secrets from the New Science of Expertise", Eduwonk, July 21, 2019, http://www.eduwonk.com/2019/07/what-the-education-sector-can-learn-from-peak-secrets-from-the-new-science-of-expertise.html
24. Knauff M, Budeck C, Wolf AG, Hamburger K. The illogicality of stock-brokers: psychological experiments on the effects of prior knowledge and belief biases on logical reasoning in stock trading. PLoS One. 2010 Oct 18;5(10):e13483. https://journals.plos.org/plosone/article?id=10.1371/journal.pone.0013483 PMID: 20976157; PMCID: PMC2956684.
25. Parr WV, Heatherbell D, White KG. Demystifying wine expertise: olfactory threshold, perceptual skill and semantic memory in expert and novice wine judges. Chem Senses. 2002 Oct;27(8):747-55. https://doi.org/10.1093/chemse/27.8.747 PMID: 12379599.
26. Robyn Dawes, *House of Cards: Psychology and Psychotherapy Built on Myth* (New York, Free Press, 1994), 13.
27. Daniel Coyle, *The Talent Code: Greatness Isn't Born. It's Grown. Here's How*, (New York, Bantam, 2009), 18.
28. Sampaio-Baptista C, Khrapitchev AA, Foxley S, Schlagheck T, Scholz J, Jbabdi S, DeLuca GC, Miller KL, Taylor A, Thomas N, Kleim J, Sibson NR, Bannerman D, Johansen-Berg H. Motor skill learning induces changes in white matter microstructure and myelination. J Neurosci. 2013 Dec 11;33(50):19499-503. https://www.jneurosci.org/content/33/50/19499
29. Michael Lantz, "Practice makes perfect? No deep practice does", Michael Lantz, Dec 19, 2018, https://www.michaellantz.net/blog/deep-practice-skill-myelin

6. Charity Is Perverse

1. Brice McKeever, "The Nonprofit Sector Brief in 2018", Urban Institute, December 13, 2018, https://nccs.urban.org/publication/nonprofit-sector-brief-2018
2. Daphne Merkin, "'Secrets of the Soul': Is Psychoanalysis Science or Is It Toast?", The New York Times, September 5, 2004, https://www.nytimes.com/2004/09/05/books/review/secrets-of-the-soul-is-psychoanalysis-science-or-is-it-toast.html
3. Steve Corbett, *When Helping Hurts: How to Alleviate Poverty Without Hurting the Poor...and Yourself*, (Chicago, Moody Publishers, 2014), 62.
4. Robert D. Lupton, *Toxic Charity: How the Church Hurts Those They Help and How to Reverse It*, (New York, HarperOne,

2011), 12.
5. Roland Bunch, *Two Ears of Corn: A Guide to People-centered Agricultural Improvement*, (Oklahoma City, World Neighbors, 1982), 18.
6. Amber Stargell, "Gold Star Charity", Catholic Charities Diocese of Toledo, October 9, 2014, https://catholiccharities nwo.org/gold-star-charity/
7. Jacques Ellul, *Money & Power*, (Downers Grove, InterVarsity Press, 1984), 112.
8. C. Andrew Doyle, *A Generous Community: Being the Church in a New Missionary Age*, (New York, Morehouse Publishing, 2015), 89.
9. Dambisa Moyo, *Dead Aid: Why Aid Is Not Working and How There Is a Better Way for Africa*, (New York, Farrar, Straus and Giroux, 2009), 44.
10. Robert D. Lupton, *Charity Detox: What Charity Would Look Like If We Cared About Results*, (New York, HarperCollins, 2015), 82.
11. World Values Survey, "V51.- Humiliating to receive money without having to work for it", World Values Survey Wave 5: 2005-2009, http://www.worldvaluessurvey.org/WVSOnline.jsp
12. Yascha Mounk, *The Age of Responsibility: Luck, Choice, and the Welfare State*, (Cambridge, Harvard University Press, 2017), 153.
13. Daniel Bennett, *A Passion for the Fatherless: Developing a God-Centered Ministry to Orphans*, (Grand Rapids, Kregel Ministry, 2011), 42.
14. Carolina Azevedo, "Haiti boosts health and education in the past decade, says new UNDP report", United Nations Development Programme, June 25, 2014, https://www.undp.org/content/undp/en/home/presscenter/pressreleases/2014/06/25/haiti-boosts-health-and-education-in-the-past-decade-says-new-undp-report.html
15. Vanessa Wijngaarden, *Dynamics Behind Persistent Images of "The Other": The Interplay between Imaginations and Interactions in Maasai Cultural Tourism*, (Münster, LIT Verlag, 2016), 258.
16. Bob Lupton, "Change is Coming", Mel Trotter Ministries, September 15, 2016, https://meltrotter.wordpress.com/2016/09/15/change-is-coming/amp/
17. John Bailey, *Journey to a Better Way: A Wesleyan Perspective on Doing Mission Better*, (Bloomington, WestBow Press, 2015), 66.
18. Katie Delp, "The Dump People", Focused Community Strategies, August 18, 2011, https://www.fcsministries.org/fcs-ministries/blog/the-dump-people
19. Bob Lupton, "Asking the Right Questions about Serving", Communities First Association, July 3, 2012, https://communitiesfirstassociation.wordpress.com/2012/07/03/asking-the-right-questions-about-serving/

20. Bob Jessop, *The Pedagogy of Economic, Political and Social Crises: Dynamics, Construals and Lessons*, (New York, Routledge, 2018), 230.

7. Common Sense Is Nonexistent

1. Nicholas Schmidle, "A Very Rare Book", The New Yorker, December 8, 2013, https://www.newyorker.com/magazine/2013/12/16/a-very-rare-book
2. Alan Cowell, "After 350 Years, Vatican Says Galileo Was Right: It Moves", The New York Times, October 31, 1992, https://www.nytimes.com/1992/10/31/world/after-350-years-vatican-says-galileo-was-right-it-moves.html
3. Leah Crane, "Vatican admits Galileo was right", New Scientist, November 7, 1992, https://www.newscientist.com/article/mg13618460-600-vatican-admits-galileo-was-right/
4. Kay Carter, *Childbed Fever: A Scientific Biography Of Ignaz Semmelweis*, (New York, Routledge, 2005), 6.
5. Ron Chernow, *Washington: A Life*, (London, Penguin Books, 2010), 807.
6. Warner J. H. (1980). "Therapeutic explanation and the Edinburgh bloodletting controversy: two perspectives on the medical meaning of science in the mid-nineteenth century". *Medical history*, 24(3), 241–258, https://doi.org/10.1017/s0025727300040308
7. Sam Harris, *The End of Faith: Religion, Terror, and the Future of Reason*, (New York, W. W. Norton & Company, 2005), 234.
8. Robert Hume, "From the handshake to the high-five: a brief history of gestures", History Extra, March 13, 2020, https://www.historyextra.com/period/ancient-greece/a-brief-history-of-gestures-from-the-handshake-to-the-high-five/
9. Ghareeb, P. A., Bourlai, T., Dutton, W., & McClellan, W. T. (2013). Reducing pathogen transmission in a hospital setting. Handshake versus fist bump: a pilot study. *The Journal of hospital infection*, 85(4), 321–323. https://doi.org/10.1016/j.jhin.2013.08.010
10. Oniya, Mobolanle & Obajuluwa, S.E. & Alade, E.T. & Oyewole, Oluwafemi. (2006). Evaluation of microorganisms transmissible through handshake. African Journal of Biotechnology. 5. 1118-1121. https://www.researchgate.net/publication/279766331_Evaluation_of_microorganisms_transmissible_through_handshake
11. Sidley P. (2006). Botched circumcisions kill 14 boys in a month. BMJ : British Medical Journal, 333(7558), 62. https://doi.org/10.1136/BMJ.333.7558.62-D

12. Boyle, G. (2015) Circumcision of Infants and Children: Short-Term Trauma and Long-Term Psychosexual Harm. Advances in Sexual Medicine, 5, 22-38. https://dx.doi.org/10.4236/asm.2015.52004
13. Jingjing Gao, Chuan Xu, Jingjing Zhang, Chaozhao Liang, Puyu Su, Zhen Peng, Kai Shi, Dongdong Tang, Pan Gao, Zhaoxiang Lu, Jishuang Liu, Lei Xia, Jiajia Yang, Zongyao Hao, Jun Zhou, Xiansheng Zhang, "Effects of Adult Male Circumcision on Premature Ejaculation: Results from a Prospective Study in China", *BioMed Research International*, vol. 2015, Article ID 417846, 7 pages, 2015. https://doi.org/10.1155/2015/417846
14. Arthur Zukerman, "56 MARRIAGE STATISTICS: 2020/2021 GLOBAL DATA, ANALYSIS & TRENDS", Compare Camp, May 31, 2020, https://comparecamp.com/marriage-statistics/
15. "Child, early and forced marriage", Government of Canada, August 20, 2020, https://www.international.gc.ca/world-monde/issues_development-enjeux_developpement/human_rights-droits_homme/child_marriage-mariages_enfants.aspx
16. Kathryn Schulz, *Being Wrong: Adventures in the Margin of Error*, (New York, HarperCollins, 2010), 4.
17. Heck, P. R., Simons, D. J., & Chabris, C. F. (2018). 65% of Americans believe they are above average in intelligence: Results of two nationally representative surveys. *PloS one*, *13*(7), e0200103. https://doi.org/10.1371/journal.pone.0200103
18. Matthew DeBord, "Americans are dangerously overconfident in their driving skills —but they're about to get a harsh reality check", Business Insider, January 25, 2018, https://www.businessinsider.com/americans-are-overconfident-in-their-driving-skills-2018-1
19. Cross, K. (1977). Not can, but will college teaching be improved? New Directions for Higher Education, 1977, 1-15. https://onlinelibrary.wiley.com/doi/10.1002/he.36919771703
20. Derek Smith, "Before Anyone Can Learn Anything, They Have to Learn to Listen", Biz Library, March 13, 2018, https://www.bizlibrary.com/blog/self-development/learn-to-listen/
21. Richard Hughes Jones, "Daniel Kahneman on the cognitive biases of entrepreneurs", RichardHughesJones.com, February 19, 2017, https://www.richardhughesjones.com/daniel-kahneman-cognitive-biases-entrepreneurs/
22. Chetan Parikh, "Making mistakes", Capital Ideas Online, March 19, 2019, https://capitalideasonline.com/wordpress/making-mistakes/
23. James MacMillan, "The principle of charity and intellectual humility", Bologna, December 13, 2019, https://jamesmacmillan.wordpress.com/2019/12/13/8791/

24. Chris Mooney, "Liberals deny science, too", The Washington Post, October 28, 2014, https://www.washingtonpost.com/news/wonk/wp/2014/10/28/liberals-deny-science-too/
25. Tom Nichols, *The Death of Expertise: The Campaign Against Established Knowledge And Why It Matters*, (New York, Oxford University Press, 2017), 130.
26. Kruger, J., & Dunning, D. (1999). Unskilled and unaware of it: how difficulties in recognizing one's own incompetence lead to inflated self-assessments. *Journal of personality and social psychology*, 77(6), 1121–1134. https://doi.org/10.1037//0022-3514.77.6.1121
27. Bertrand Russell, *Mortals and Others*, (New York, Routledge, 1975), 204.
28. Kevin Simler, "Crony Beliefs", Melting Asphalt, November 2, 2016, https://meltingasphalt.com/crony-beliefs/
29. Adam Grant, *Think Again: The Power of Knowing What You Don't Know*, (New York, Viking, 2021), 60.
30. Bruce R. Caron, "You do science. Do you know science?", OpenScientist, March 2021, https://doi.org/10.21428/8bbb7f85.e33fa261
31. Charlotte Lydia Riley, *The Free Speech Wars: How Did We Get Here and Why Does It Matter?*, (Manchester, Manchester University Press, 2020), 97.
32. Greg Koukl, *Tactics: A Game Plan for Discussing Your Christian Convictions*, (Grand Rapids, Zondervan, 2009), 51.
33. Richard Dawkins, *The God Delusion*, (New York, Mariner Books, 2008), 320.
34. Dan McMinn, "We are all wrong about many things", Reflections on Life and Leadership, April, 2021, https://donmcminn.com/2021/04/we-are-all-wrong/
35. Dwayne Brown, "How One Man Convinced 200 Ku Klux Klan Members To Give Up Their Robes", NPR, August 20, 2017, https://www.npr.org/2017/08/20/544861933/how-one-man-convinced-200-ku-klux-klan-members-to-give-up-their-robes
36. Arain, M., Haque, M., Johal, L., Mathur, P., Nel, W., Rais, A., Sandhu, R., & Sharma, S. (2013). Maturation of the adolescent brain. *Neuropsychiatric disease and treatment*, 9, 449–461. https://doi.org/10.2147/NDT.S39776
37. Joseph Campellone, "Understanding the Teen Brain", University of Rochester Medical Center, https://www.urmc.rochester.edu/encyclopedia/content.aspx?ContentTypeID=1&ContentID=3051
38. Jonathan Fields, *Uncertainty: Turning Fear and Doubt into Fuel for Brilliance*, (Toronto, Penguin, 2011), 192.
39. Charles Renouvier, Essais de Critique Générale, Deuxième Essai, Vol. 1: Traité de Psychologie Rationnelle d'Après les Principes du Criticisme, (London, Forgotten Books, 1912), 366.

40. Bo Jinn, *Illogical Atheism: A Comprehensive Response to the Contemporary Freethinker from a Lapsed Agnostic*, (Scotts Valley, Divided Line Publishing, 2013), 307.
41. William Lane Craig, "The New Atheism and Five Arguments for God", Reasonable Faith, https://www.reasonablefaith.org/writings/popular-writings/existence-nature-of-god/the-new-atheism-and-five-arguments-for-god/
42. Mark Morford, "37 percent of people completely lost", SFGATE, March 12, 2013, https://blog.sfgate.com/morford/2013/03/12/37-percent-of-people-completely-lost/
43. Scott Youngren, "Why belief in unicorns is more logical than atheism", God Evidence, August 7, 2019, https://godevidence.com/2019/08/belief-in-unicorns/
44. Ayn Rand, Atlas Shrugged, (New York, Signet, 2005), 1017.

This Is Your Last Chance

1. J.D. Roth, "Overcoming Uncertainty", Get Rich Slowly, September 30, 2011, https://www.getrichslowly.org/overcoming-uncertainty/
2. John Koenig, "sonder", The Dictionary of Obscure Sorrows, Jul 22, 2012, https://www.dictionaryofobscuresorrows.com/post/23536922667/sonder
3. Maria Popova, "The Secret of Life from Steve Jobs in 46 Seconds", Brain Pickings, https://www.brainpickings.org/2011/12/02/steve-jobs-1995-life-failure/
4. Mark Manson, *Everything Is F*cked: A Book About Hope*, (New York, Harper, 2019), 157.
5. Murube, Juan. (2009). Hypotheses on the Development of Psychoemotional Tearing. The ocular surface. 7. 171-5. https://www.sciencedirect.com/science/article/abs/pii/S1542012412701842
6. Amos Doornbos, "Thinking in Decades", This is Amos, July 14, 2020, https://thisisamos.com/2020/07/14/thinking-in-decades/
7. Mark Manson, "The Uncomfortable Truth", Life Advice That Doesn't Suck, https://markmanson.net/the-uncomfortable-truth
8. Musashi Miyamoto, *The Book of Five Rings*, (Boston, Shambhala Publications, 2002), 40.
9. Viktor E. Frankl, Man's Search for Meaning (Boston, Beacon Press, 2006), 65.
10. Holly Richardson, "Don't think your personality is permanent", The Salt Lake Tribune, June 12, 2020, https://www.sltrib.com/opinion/commentary/2020/06/12/holly-richardson-dont/

11. Adam Grant, *Originals: How Non-Conformists Move the World*, (New York, Penguin Books, 2016), 91.

Manufactured by Amazon.ca
Acheson, AB

15460239R00096